13⁵⁰

From INTEGRITY
Edited by Angel

VOLUME
2

RAISING
YOUR
CHILDREN

ANGELUS PRESS

2918 TRACY AVENUE, KANSAS CITY, MISSOURI 64109
(816) 753-3150 ◆ FAX (816) 753-3557

Library of Congress Cataloging-in-Publication Data

Raising your children
    p. cm.
  "From Integrity the magazine"
  ISBN 0-935952-27-6 (pbk.)
   1. Child rearing–Religious aspects–Catholic Church.
2. Christian ethics–Catholic authors. 3. Children–Religious Life.
I. Integrity (100 Mile House, B.C. : 1989).
BX2351. R35 1995
248.8'45–dc20   95-43810
                                       CIP

ANGELUS PRESS

2918 TRACY AVENUE
KANSAS CITY, MISSOURI 64109
PHONE (816) 753-3150
FAX (816) 753-3557
ORDER LINE 1-800-966-7337

ISBN 0-935952-27-6
FIRST PRINTING—December 1995

Printed in the United States of America

CONTENTS

FOREWORD

One can scarcely find a pope in the last 200 years that has not written something on the family. When Pope Leo XIII was asked which of his many encyclicals he considered to be the most important, he responded giving them in this order: First, *On Christian Philosophy*, to restore Catholic thought in society and the universities (built on Thomism); Second, *On Human Liberty*, to re-emphasize that *only* the *Catholic* truth will make nations and people free; Third, *On Christian Marriage and Family*, to build a Catholic society, the "building blocks" must be solid; Fourth, *On Freemasonry*, to alarm the entire world of its deceits and naturalistic principles, that will destroy societies and families; Fifth, *On Civil Government*, to re-emphasize the union of Church and State and their relationships for the true common good; Sixth, *On the Christian Constitution of States*, to remind "Caesar," he <u>too</u> has the duty to render to God what is God's, and help his people get to heaven; Seventh, *On Socialism*, to stress that economics, too, must be governed by the virtues of justice and charity; Eighth, *On the Rights and Duties of Capital and Labor*; and Ninth, *On Christian Citizenship*, to uphold the true ideal of a true society, yes, a vision!

All these together form a whole doctrinal body giving

obvious importance to the family. Why so much focus on the family? No doubt, all the popes, like Leo XIII, foresaw that the family would soon be the target of Satan, as the coming anti-family U.N. Conference in Beijing, China, proves.

What are we to do? Simply, our duties of state (Our Lady of Fatima), and keep our Catholic feet on the ground. In this latest compendium of *Integrity* articles by various authors, fathers will discover their important role in God's plan, from business meetings and feeding the family, to leading the family rosary and meal prayers. What of you mothers? St. Paul already canonizes you! "The woman shall be saved through childbearing." You are the heart of the home, the warmth and light of the homelife, and in these pages you will find sound advice on "beating in harmony" with the head, and, *both together*, on raising the children God sends you. The topics are vast and touch on many practical applications of the Faith with so much simplicity and common sense.

We belong to that Family of the Blessed Trinity already! How? By our union with the Mystical Body of Christ (through the Catholic Faith and sanctifying grace!) and this Body will be glorified with Her Head: "Eye hath not seen, ear hath not heard, nor hath it entered into the heart of man what God hath prepared for those that love Him!" (I Cor. 2:9). Those saintly popes are watching you, countless parent-saints are cheering you on and even envy you! So dear parents, go, grow, and glow with the graces from your Nuptial Blessing, and may the request of Mother Church, after this "valley of tears," be yours!

> May the God of Abraham, the God of Isaac, and the God of Jacob be with you, and may He fulfill His blessing in you: that you may see your children's children

even to the third and fourth generation, and thereafter may you have Life Everlasting, by the grace of Our Lord Jesus Christ: Who with the Father and the Holy Ghost liveth and reigneth, God, forever and ever. Amen. (Nuptial Blessing after *Benedicamus Domino.*)

Rev. Fr. David Hewko
Feast of the Holy Name of Mary, 1995

Our Infantile Paralysis

Marion Mitchell Stancioff

"Unless ye be as great big children you shall nowise enter into the kingdom of our modern world. Unless ye remain at a mental stage of perpetual adolescence ye shall be cast into outer darkness where there is nothing but maladjustment and neuroses." These are the basic texts we live by, and *Magna Carta* of the education we give our young.

The difference between a child and a man lies in two things: in what it wants and how it wants it; in its interests and its activities. The child is parasitical, acquisitive, wanting to take to itself (to the extent of stuffing it in its mouth) everything it sees. The man is independent, constructive, prepared to give as well as take. When we become men, the Apostle says, we put away childish things. Yet a glance around us shows that we cling to them, and by our example encourage our children to do so. We make a show of infantile eagerness to see a game, and express exaggerated disappointment when we fail to find tickets. Instead, we should be training the children—in whom such eagerness is comprehensible—to curb such manifestations of ecstacy and of re-

gret. Our living habits are those of babyhood. We eat soft
food and we drink soft drinks. Milk, the proper food of infants, has become the staple diet of an aging nation, and
what was once called the staff of life has become highgrade
blotting paper which could sustain no one for very long.
Our teeth never encounter a crust and rarely do we bite a
fruit, preferring the baby way of drinking it from a bottle.
We seldom walk more than a few blocks and are careful to
give the children carfare lest they tire their little legs. We ply
these babes with pocket money so they may never have to
resist the desire for a sweet, for "we know how hard it is not
to have what you want," and we do not appear to know how
good it is *not* to have what you want. We think we are doing
our duty by our descendants when we teach them the means
to acquire what they want instead of teaching them not to
want it. (What far-reaching results such a teaching would
have on our industry! For we are indeed a nation of shop-
pers.) We think that teaching them to be successes, in games,
in sex, in business, is all the education they require to be
fully equipped grown-ups. We are actually only teaching them
new games to play with, fresh toys when the teddy bears and
trains get tiresome. Young people are encouraged to be creative with clay and cloth, with paint and plastiline, with every material except the one always available and always free
of charge, their own natures. They are given the tools of any
craft they have in mind to try their hand at it, but they are
not given the instruments of thought their minds could use-
fully handle. They are thrown a few haphazard ideas to play
with which make no more sense of the cosmos than worn
out bits of a jigsaw puzzle. So in discouragement they turn
their minds away from its God-given purpose of thought
and busy their brains with problems of sport or money-making.

We encourage our young to live in a world of make-believe because we feel that it is safer than the world of reality. We systematically teach children to live for play and are surprised when in times of crisis they act like children. It is true that "all work and no play makes Jack a dull boy," but it is equally true that "all play and no work makes John a dumb jerk." If sports were just a youthful passion, we could willingly condone it, but when we see them become the favorite topic of middle-aged professors and elderly statesmen, when we hear ministers of religion discussing the merits of a halfback or the subtleties of a pitcher, we recognize that theirs is no temporary intrusion into the world of childhood, but a frantic flight from facts.

This is comprehensible enough. The twentieth century has many facts it were pleasanter not to face. We have taken refuge from the things we cannot entirely forget, the wars and the depressions, the concentration camps and torture chambers, in the make-believe world of sports. At a time when honor stands dishonored and fair play is an antiquated notion, we gladly fly to the artificial world of sport where

CRIB OR COUCH

**Psychiatrists are a wealthy class
Much frequented by ladies,
Since housewives started wanting furs
Instead of wanting babies.**

honor and fair play are enduring slogans. In a world where in great part law is lawless and justice just ignored, the rules of the game create a comforting sense of security. Is it any wonder we encourage our children to inhabit a world so much more to our own liking than the world we adults have made? But is there any hope of re-making the real world in a more tolerable pattern if we leave the young in their play-world? They will be called out of it roughly enough one day, so should we not lead them out of it now and help them to grow up?

They Need Light to Grow

The first requisite for the ripening of the seed is light—that is, in the case of man, a true conception of his function in the universe.

Both in the animal order and the human order the end of puberty is the beginning of maturity. What prevents us from ripening is the underlying idea of our own animality. Maturity means ripeness for a purpose. In the vegetable and animal order it means fitness for physical reproduction. In the human order it not only means fitness for reproduction and the entailed physical responsibilities—nurture and defense of a family. In man or woman it is a fitness for moral responsibilities, for spiritual care, which indicate maturity.

In healthy periods of civilization minority ends with the end of puberty. No matter how unpleasant the world may seem or how little the youth may care to face it, he does so because he is indoctrinated with his obligations to his fellow men and their common Maker. In the past kings took over the reins of government at an age when our boys are as yet ineligible to drive a motor vehicle. In the heyday of the Sorbonne, of Oxford, of Bologne, men were graduated from these universities at an age when our boys are getting ready for senior year in high school. It may be argued that they did not know as much then; and it is true that in the exact sciences there were fewer facts to know. But in philosophy and letters few will deny their superiority nor the clarity of their reasoning and the maturity of their judgment. There were foolish youths then as always, but thought was taken seriously in its own right and not simply as a means to a high-salaried job. The mind was trained in the university and the character was trained in the home or the school and the young people were prepared for the struggles and the stress of life. The schools now have no time for character formation, nor standards of measuring maturity. Only a mature person can judge of maturity and only after a certain amount of all-round personal contact. In crowded schools the busy teachers cannot have enough personal contact to judge them. So intelligence tests are substituted as a basis of assessment. A boy I know, who comes from a literate home, after having dawdled over Latin and having lazed over Greek for a few years, entered a high school and was given the usual intelligence test. His parents, who had suffered from his refusal to work, his rejection of responsibility, and general immaturity of character, were very astonished when they found they were being congratulated on having "the most mature boy in the school, years ahead of his age." These conclusions had been arrived at on the basis of a wide vocabulary which he had acquired by no effort of his own. If educators do not know what maturity is, how can the student work toward it?

The educators do feel, however, that there is something lacking in their products, so they drag out the hothouse process of education—and with it the cherished adolescent atmosphere—as long as possible. This long postponement of living brings, not ripeness, but decay. Responsibilities are so long deferred that the college boy has lost the zest to ponder them. Nor is there any chance he will ever want to unless he is given a good reason for doing so. It is not enough to be able to reproduce ourselves. We must know why we are doing it. If the reason is not good, youth cannot be blamed for running away from reality. Unless we believe that there is "no proportion between the pains of this life and the joy to come" then logically death becomes the one great unpleasantness never to be mentioned, old age a nasty condition of decay to be disguised as well as possible, and only the years of health and beauty are worth living at all. If we look upon ourselves simply as intellectual beasts, then there is no maturity beyond the physiological ripeness of puberty, nor is there a need of any.

They Need Pure Air

The second requisite for the growth of a seed is pure air. Youth needs the atmosphere of a sound society.

The various manifestations of our unsoundness, economic, domestic, educational, have been often enough examined. Self-evident proof of our unsoundness is the extraordinary rise of insanity in the last thirty or forty years. Either life is worse than it used to be or we are less fit to cope with it. Perhaps we are not teaching the facts of life to the children, or not the right facts. We do teach them something, I admit. They know quite a bit about fetal development and coital incompatibility. But these are only part of facts about parts of life. They are not learning the fundamental facts which have to do with good and evil, courage and cowardice, intellectual honesty and love and fidelity, the need for pain, the dignity of death. They are only learning to avoid learning them—and at this we are excellent teachers. If they don't succeed in avoiding facts, if life insists on violently embracing them, they develop painful trauma and are incurably maimed. Experiences which used to build character now build mental institutions. Our young people cannot ripen in a society that is unsound. They are immature because our old people are, and our old people dare not grow up because the alternative to childishness is despair.

They Need Love

The third requisite for the ripening of the seed is moisture. Love is needed to keep the spirit from drying up, and to nourish its growth.

We hear a great deal about the love we owe our children. Even the intellectual-beast school concedes love to have teleological value. But there are many kinds of love. The love we shower on our children should be of the highest quality, which, like "the quality of mercy is not strained." It is natural and simple and flows from the heart and not from the mother-craft book. It does not tie children to apron strings nor does it try to appear indifferent to their ventures. It lets them take reasonable risks for it entrusts them to their Mother in Heaven. Thus as they grow in stature they will also grow in courage, in prudence and in grace, with no shadow of momism or "father complex" to darken their paths. The example of truly mature love between parents is the best antitoxin to the hysterical love of the magazines and the movies. Living and growing under the wings of such an affection can make straight the paths of the next generation, can keep its feet off the tortuous and thorny way of worldly loves.

But how shall children learn to grow up in homes where their elders envy them their youth? Where mothers try to grow down to their daughters, where paunchy "pops" call themselves "one of the boys," and white-haired grandmothers bedeck themselves in bridesmaids' finery and chatter of "we girls." If the young see around them idolatry of youth, they cannot be expected to renounce any characteristic of that perfect state.

Many parents are infinitely careful to let no breath of authority taint the beautiful big-sister and big-brother relationship with their children. They try so hard just to be boys and girls together lest the young think they are telling them what to do; they keep their own experience out of their way until the youngsters, finding the job of making decisions too big for them, start to shirk it as we are shirking ours. They must know that there is an authority, but a loving one which prefers cooperation to duress. In united families there is cooperation in all things; the children told of difficulties and their help secured. They share in the responsibilities and in the joys of the whole group. A child should feel that everything he does affects the welfare of the group as a whole. Parents who make sacrifices in order that their little boys may have as many ice cream cones as the Jones' boy are silly. If they think he must have everything, he will think so too and will expect the world to give it to him when they are gone. Parents have plenty of sacrifices to make in serious things. "But the poor child cannot be expected to know that there are more serious things than sundaes..." No, of course not—if he is never told. Most parents know, but do not always remember, that it is more important to sacrifice leisure than money, better to have a good game together once in a while than to let Junior go much to the movies, that it is more useful to teach him to make things than to give him money to buy them, and to teach him to rely for entertainment as much as possible on his own resources—in general to be independent and self-reliant. "But we do teach our boy to be independent," cry some parents, "We let him sell papers and help out at the store." This, however, is usually done to give him a sense of business, and not for any serious motive such as helping with the home expenses. Or it is done in order that the youngster should have more petty cash with which to indulge his whims. That is teaching him what he already knows, to live for himself, not for others. It is not only we who must love our children to the point of unselfishness, but they who must love us, not for our sakes but for theirs, or they will never grow up. And we alone can teach them this.

Another means of keeping close to them, provided we begin early enough, before they can read, is to read interesting books to them, instead of letting them look at the comics while we enjoy our deserved and longed-for book. This habit will form an invaluable link between parent and child. It is a means of touching on serious topics which never come up in the ordinary course of talk. It will open doors which nothing else can unlock and a subtle means of help and guidance. It is all the more necessary because of the horizontal division of the United States' humanity into age groups which does so much to prevent a true exchange of ideas between generations. This arbitrary division is, perhaps, more than any other single factor, responsible for the inanity of so much youthful talk—and consequently of youthful thinking as well. Instead of listening to their grandfathers' friends discussing matters of the moment and talking of serious topics with men of their fathers' generation, these youths are condemned by convention to spend their leisure listening to the drivel or the eventually wearisome wit of fellow teenagers. It is partly the smallness of modern apartments which breaks up the family group, prevents mixed gatherings of friends and leads to the club-life at the drug store. It is chiefly because parents have lost touch with their children and think they don't want them around and fly the premises in a panic. Actually, intelligent young people are frequently flattered to find the older

people talking to them seriously so parents might find it re-
warding to stay and be human. The restriction of social life
to contact with persons as ignorant as oneself is certainly
fatal to conversation, that is, true conversation, which is an
exchange of ideas and experiences and not just small talk. It
is equally fatal to mutual development. Nor is the drug store,
where so many of these meetings take place, a stimulation
for the mind. These youngsters sitting high on their stools,
looking over into slops, surrounded by shelves bulging with
bubblegum and beauty creams instead of books, fill one with
compassion for a generation which has been helped by its
elders to grow but not to grow "up."

They Need Good Soil

The fourth requisite for the ripening of a seed is soil. It
doesn't always have to be a fine loam. Grit and sand and
gravel are just as necessary as leafmold for most plants. They
provide the minerals which give firmness to the stalk and let
the roots get a good grip.

It is a truism that boys who have had to struggle since
their early youth frequently grow into bigger men than some
sheltered youths. Even though they may not be as developed
intellectually, their characters have been matured by difficulties and responsibilities for which there is no effective
substitute. The generation that grew up in the Depression
are for the most part far less childish than their parents or
their children. But even those who do not come up the hard
way can find plenty of salutary hardness in life if they are
trained to face it. Even so apparently small a thing as resistance against group pressure in school, college or office will
make a youth into a man. It is very difficult to teach a child
the need for this. If we harp on it too much we may make
him a hopeless conformist. The pressure of the school group

is so strong that the family has to wage constant war to save the child from the casting mold. It is very uncomfortable for child and for parents. The resistance is easier to induce in large families where there is an opposite-group pressure. It is easier still if several like-minded families live in the same neighborhood, send their children to the same school. Every family that resists the conventional foolishness makes it that much easier for others. But this being "different" is never easy, and with some children it is not possible at all. But let us not be scared by the trauma we hear so much about. Wounds are natural to man and he must learn to heal. Without some cuts and bruises no lad ever developed strong muscles or sound bones or lived to reach maturity.

Why Don't Catholics Mature?

We have seen that human development follows the same lines as that of plants, requiring the light of a clear belief, the atmosphere of a healthy society, an affectionate home life which is like life-giving water, and the soil of hardship and difficulty in order to attain fruition.

Now why is it that so many Catholic boys are permanent adolescents? Their religion gives them a true conception of their function in the cosmos, they were raised for the most part in unbroken homes, lived in a Catholic atmosphere and did not entirely escape difficulties. What then is lacking?

We Catholics are trying to "pass." We are not prepared to live our religion in all its implications of prayer and penance and poverty. Perhaps it is because these things seem un-American even a little psychopathic, and because we think we must be successes—like everyone else—in order to advertise God. We want to "pass," want to be all things to all men, so we pass away without having been very much to any man or anything much to God.

We teach our young Catholics the ways and means of being as indistinguishable as possible from the herd. On Sundays and days of obligation they sidle out from the bunch and go sheepishly to church. On Fridays they avoid meat, and they even avoid blacklisted movies if they can. But wherever there is no specific interdiction, wherever it is a question of character rather than commandment, they happily follow the herd. When our children are small they must wear the same type of shirt as the rest, when adolescent they must kiss the same type of girl. Some Catholic boys take their religious instruction seriously enough to have qualms about necking, but dare not brave opinion by taking a girl out without kissing her or going out in a group of avowed non-neckers, so prefer to sink their "difference" in whiskey or in beer. The fear of lechery explains a great deal of the drinking amongst Catholic boys. If fornication can only be fought with drunkenness there is something wrong with the way our religion is being taught. Too many Catholic institutions teach a watered-down Catholicism which stimulates no one to the heroism necessary for everyday life. Christ's disciples were so filled with the Holy Ghost that observers thought them drunk though it was early in the morning. The Holy Spirit is indeed such a stimulant that no other spirits are required. Obviously those boys have not been kept close enough to the Holy Ghost to feel the tongues of fire or they wouldn't be falling back on the passing warmth of alcohol.

And since there is a certain light that lighteth every man that cometh into the world, the fraud of watered-down religion is in the long run detected by the young. Those who do not drown their disappointment at life in drink, deaden it with business or wear it down with exercise, and some as we know, give up either their religion or their sanity.

I once asked a priest who had taught for many years in a high-grade Catholic college why so many of the young people they graduated were lamentably childish, why the vast majority seemed incapable of self-government or even of serious discussion. He said sadly that a large proportion of the teachers were of the same mental age as their pupils. The faculty members had so long simulated an exclusive interest in sports, had so long eschewed serious subjects, had tried so hard to speak the language of youth, that this had become their only tongue—spoken even amongst themselves. It is not with the gift of such a tongue that the Holy Ghost endows His faithful, nor will it suffice to communicate the glory of God. Once when I said to a young priest who had spoken very familiar, loving words about God: "Father, it's good to hear you talk like that. Most of the priests I know do not," he answered, "We can't often do so, even among priests; at the seminary the conversation was almost always about something else..." and his voice was full of sorrow.

Youth, therefore, eternal youth is everyone's ideal. It is the cult not only of the ignorant, but of the instructed, since most of these believe only in the here-and-now and those who believe in more dare not behave as if they did. The educators of various schools are satisfied to get more and more expensive kindergarten equipment for the establishments where they condition the young for this playful world. Clerics of diverse faiths are satisfied to improve playroom facilities for their flocks and let them substitute generosity of purse for generosity of heart and mind; letting them relax thereafter in the pharisaical conviction that they have done their share.

Until this attitude changes our young will not. It is not without significance that the one genuine myth creation of the twentieth century is the figure of the child who refused to grow up, the boy who escaped into a private dreamland in order to avoid being a man. Peter Pan, coupling the name of the Apostle with the name of the faun, the animal all-god of antiquity, is a valid symbol of our time. A vestigial Christianity grafted upon an antique survival with the Faith drained out of both, is a true summary of our civilization. The imaginary pipes lead us in our scamper back to the happy dreamland of nursery thoughts from which we shall soon be awakened with an iron sound.

How Modern Man Became Merry

Carol Robinson

Retracing briefly the history of modern man, we find
that the Acquisitive Society was superseded by the Leisure
State, which in turn gave way to the great Age of Penance
just ended.

It was during the early acquisitive age that the institutions of society gradually were oriented to money-making as
a final end, refashioned from the old Christian pattern to
the service of mammon. Not everyone swung over to the
love of money, but the leaders of society did, and they exercised a sort of personal monasticism in the pursuit of that
end.

Since we are concerned here chiefly with recreation rather
than economics, let us pause to examine the leisure-time
activities of the acquisitive man. The outstanding characteristic was secularization. The play of that period was no more
related to God than was the work. The holidays were patri-
otic land bank holidays, not saints' days. Men golfed sol-

emnly, with an awareness of the physical benefits to be derived from a day in the open air after a week at the office desk. They traveled much abroad during the intermittent periods of peace, for cultural and business reasons, engaging chiefly in sightseeing. They enjoyed the theater, concerts, card playing, and what they used to call the "books of the month." This is the early acquisitive period, remember, when men still seemed able to hold to the good natural order, when it looked as though, having abandoned Christianity (except for occasional lip service), men could maintain a cultured pagan standard of life.

As the rich grew richer, but not happier, the poor were regimented increasingly, by the natural progress of an unnatural system of industrial mass production, into a propertyless, proletarian condition in which they were virtually robots. It is unlikely that the masses of the people, with their Christian heritage, could have been persuaded (as the leaders were) that money could buy happiness. But they did discover that in an industrial society money can buy quite a bit of oblivion. The more industrialized society became, so much the more intolerable life became for the masses of the people. The more intolerable life became, the more industrial production was diverted from physical necessities (such as housing, basic clothing, and food) to instruments of entertainment and diversion. Men slaved monotonously to make the television sets which would make their monotonous lives tolerable. They sold themselves into the chain gangs of the automobile plants so as to earn enough money to buy an automobile. A sort of ratio persisted between the demands of a dehumanized population for escape and the sacrifice of mind, will, energy and talents which went into making the latest escape device; the former always running a little ahead of the latter. Naturally the majority of men did not realize that they were busy tightening the noose around their own necks. They looked to a paradise of pleasure just beyond their reach. It was called the Leisure State.

The theory of the Leisure State was exactly the opposite of the Christian theory of life and work. "Man is born to labor as the bird to fly," one of the contemporary Popes said. The Leisure State denied this, contending instead that man is made to play and will be able to do so almost all the time as soon as science has made work unnecessary.

It never did come about, as the supporters of the Leisure State anticipated, that the work week was reduced to five or ten hours. Instead it hit a brief forty-hour low and then rose again until it reached a seven-day week. However, leisure as an ideal was certainly enthroned. The entertainment industry ran into the billions of dollars. Huge amphitheaters, sport gardens, stadiums, gymnasiums, playgrounds, race tracks, provided the setting for spectator, professionalized sports on a gigantic scale. Movies, radio and television were ubiquitous. Escape literature flooded the newsstands. Although the work week did not decrease but increased, the invention of labor-saving devices made it possible for men to divide their time between mechanical office or factory work and sedentary amusements. It freed women from what they liked to call the "drudgery" of housework, so that they, too, could become parts of the machinery in offices and factories. Then they too had to escape from their dehumanized existence into the temporary oblivion of drink or lust or the movie house.

As long as it could, by fair means or foul, the Leisure State refused to recognize its major problem, but in the end there came about a sustained national crisis. People were bored. Everyone was bored. One would put the greatest mechanical wonder of science down in any man's home—

say a machine by which he could pick up a chance conversation in the streets of Shanghai, or something that would transport a man to the emperor's Palace in Tokyo in three minutes. Our good man would but yawn, or say, "Yeah, it's a nice color," or "What's this dial for?"

The government tried in every way to awaken people's interest in anything at all besides relaxation. There resulted a rash of things such as garden clubs ("Nature is the most fascinating thing on earth. Just wait until you have grown your own little radishes!"). But there were no takers, except for a few eccentrics who were so fascinated they began to worship nature and developed a ritual cult of the wheat germ. Again the government tried interesting the citizens in "worthy books," masterpieces of literature and philosophy beloved of other ages. No go! The majority was indifferent. A few intellectuals became sophists, and went around trying to tell people how much they had studied of other people's own ideas without having attained to any major convictions of their own.

The breakdown of the Leisure State came about through some Catholics who decided one day to take the Church seriously and literally. There had been a lot of talk about doing penance and it finally occurred to one of the faithful that that might mean him. He managed to round up a small group to consider the matter. Right off they saw the difficulty. "If we stopped consuming so much, what would happen to the system?...It doesn't so much matter about us, but suppose it became a fad?...Suppose people lost their confidence in an ever-increasing standard of living?" But they decided to try it anyhow.

Following the theory (as they read in a spiritual book) that it is more humble to accept the penances God has sent one than to seek extraordinary ones, they decided to accept their monotonous work as penance. "Forgive us, O Lord, for we have forsaken Thee and sought after money," they repeated in their hearts as they set the screws in the radios or dropped the cookies into the designated places in the special fancy-assortment boxes. "Have pity on us, Christ, and make us men again," they chanted in unison, unheard by others over the din of the machines. "We offer our sufferings for the souls of this generation....Accept them, O Lord," prayed seven young women in a Coca-Cola bottling plant, over the Musak in the background.

It naturally followed that the penitents abstained from the escapist joys of their co-workers in the evening. "If our work is going to be penance, then we must face the reality of it and not try to deaden the pain." They took to praying quite a bit at night and gathering in small groups (their number was spreading) for mutual support and encouragement. The more penance they did, the more they became aware of the need for penance. They began to see how wide was the gulf by which modern man had separated himself from God. They saw souls all around them in danger of everlasting fire.

"Let us fast for our fellow workers," they decided. So they did, limiting themselves to dry bread, fresh fruit, hash and boiled potatoes. And then a funny thing happened. "Have you noticed," said one penitent to another some weeks later, "how truly delicious are boiled potatoes?" "That's odd," said another, "I never liked hash in my life until now, and last night's meal was more delicious than ever I found the latest taste sensation in my days of culinary delights. My meals have a zest."

A similar thing occurred when the penitents started practicing custody of the eyes. All one Lent they went about with eyes cast down, abstaining from video, window shopping, advertisement reading, and even from viewing the budding trees, the floral displays in Radio City, the blue heavens by day or the starlit skies at night. "The single tulip I saw on Easter Sunday," testified one, "filled my whole being with its loveliness and the day with blissful joy."

So, too, with sound. Solitude and silence restored the power to appreciate delicate harmony (as opposed to the unmelodious imitation of factory noises of the latest symphonies and the maudlin sentimentality of popular crooning). Gregorian chant for the first time had the power to lift their hearts to holy things.

Delight shone increasingly on the faces of the penitents, whose numbers had now swollen to the proportions of a minor movement. Quite a number of people were being jarred out of their lethargy. Then a new matter came up.

A middle-aged man spoke up at one of the weekly meetings of one of the original groups: "I've been in this penitential movement three years, fellow Christians. I offer up the monotony of my work to Christ, same as all of you. You will remember we started doing this in order to make a virtue of necessity. Do you realize that we have inadvertently destroyed the necessity of our own slavery? Since we don't love automobiles, airplanes, television sets and three-inch steaks, we can live on very little. Must we continue to be robots or do you think God would be pleased to have us lead our fellowmen toward a more simple life, a more human work?"

That was the beginning of the end of industrialization as a pattern of society, and marked the death knell of the Leisure State. People began to form in small Christian communities and started to work at crafts, farming, and apostolic ventures. As their common Christian life and creative work grew, so their joy increased and overflowed into simple songs and dances. Sunday was again observed and men came to celebrate the holy days instead of the secular holidays. Where formerly there had been a military parade as the focal point of the day's festivities, now there was a religious procession, not so martial but twice as colorful, and inviting the participation of the whole community. Not the parade ground, the town hall, or the local tavern, but the parish church, and especially the Cathedral, became the center of social activities. Tourism gave way to pilgrimages which united men of all nations not only in prayer and penance but also in an exchange of conversation and culture, in song, discussion and dance. People began to have fun in families. Parents found new delight in their children. Laughter rang out in the streets. Through the death of mortification came a life of new joy.

That's how modern man became merry.

Why Bring Up the Child?

Elizabeth Williams

It is apparent that interest in the child is on the upswing. Perhaps it is a strange thing when we take into consideration the fact that the child is becoming more and more rare. But I suppose it is this very fact that moves every parent to desire to produce the perfect specimen, and every pediatrician to give forth with the perfect pointers on how this is done.

The *New York Times* has a special weekly page called *The Parent and the Child*, and so has every other newspaper. In magazines there are numerous articles giving ideas good, bad, and indifferent on child training. It is quite a business—this child care and development. And it is being given over more and more into the hands of specialists. Nursery schools insure the child of expert care at an early age. Even before that, while he is still an infant, development clinics determine whether his mental progress is normal. And even before he is born, there are special courses and classes for both his father and mother. For they, too, must become specialists, and since too often they are specializing in one child, it is impossible for them to learn by experience.

All these sessions, courses and columns are concerned with the "how" of child-upbringing. The question, "Why bring up the child?" may sound facetious, yet it is the root of the problem. And no one bothers discussing it. Planned parenthood associates have fully discussed "Why have the Child?" and resolved this question with many answers why *not* to have him. But everyone knows that once a child is here you have to do *something* about him, and child psychology is the *something done*.

"Why bring up the child?" may sound like a ridiculous question to Christians, and they have every right to think so, since the simplest of them knows the right answer. But since so few of us are Christian today (in the places where it counts most—in our heart and our heads), we may do well to think this question over and examine its implications fully. To do this we have to know the origin of the child, his purpose in life, his place in the scheme of things, and his nature.

The importance of these matters was brought home to me recently when I listened to a lecture by a Catholic pediatrician who omitted them all from his talk. Perhaps he felt they were implied in what he said, and charity makes us believe that at least personally he is aware of their importance. But their omission reduced his lecture to the naturalistic, secularistic level, and made "the happy life" he envisioned for the child seem the work of a sincere pagan scientist. I am using his lecture as an example not because I think either he or the lecture is unusual, but because they are illustrative of the tendency today to submit the child completely to scientific "psychological" control, without bothering to consider the philosophical tenets which are at the basis of the psychology. The same doctor had said on a previous occasion, "I subscribe fully to the theory of Dr. Gesell* on child development." It would be more to the point if he had said (or could say) first: "I subscribe fully to the doctrines of Christ."

We shall return to his lecture presently, but let us first consider the:

Origin of the Child

I was glancing through a magazine once when I caught these words, out of their context I admit, but in any context they would be surprising: "The proud parents believed the child was providential, but the doctors assured them it was an entirely natural conception." It is obvious that the poor author of that sentence doesn't know what "providential" means. He evidently thinks it means extraordinary or miraculous or unnatural. We who know that it means none of these things, know also that there is nothing essentially contradictory between the ideas of providence and of nature. The wings of a bird are providential, so are the leaves on a tree. Every child is providential. The fact that his conception is natural, and that God makes use of secondary causes for His creation, does not take it away from the realm of His providence. God, Who directly creates the soul of the child, provides for the making of his body in a way that should fill his parents with awe. Co-creation, however much it can be explained as a natural biological function, is providential.

Purpose of the Child

When we have once established God as the Prime Originator of the child, we can go on to reason correctly as to

---

* Dr. Gesell was an eminent specialist at the Child Clinic at Yale. He wrote many books, including *The Infant and the Child in the Culture of Today*. Catholics were quite impressed with him.

what is the purpose of the child and what is his destiny. The pediatrician I mentioned above, who was lecturing on how to make the child secure and well-adjusted and a success in life, concluded thusly: "If we do all these things, we shall fit the child to take his place in modern society." In this, his last sentence, the doctor made mention of the thing that we must thrash out first. He discussed completely *how* to raise the child. He took for granted that our aim in so doing is to make the child a success in modern society. Is it? That is the question we have to decide. As Christians we know the child is here to know, love and serve God in this world in order to reach his supernatural destiny in the next. If modern society is in harmony with the law of God, if the temporal order today is ordained to the eternal order, and if fellowship with the people of modern society is a preparation for fellowship with the saints, then well and good. Let us train our children to take their place in modern society, and to be a success in it. But if modern society is ordained to the service of man and has no goal outside itself, if fitting into it means learning to ignore God and adore material progress, if being a success in it means taking scandal at the folly of Christ, then why train our children to take their places in it? Whittle down their intellect so that they will be content to know creatures instead of God; constrain their hearts so they will love self, instead of expanding with an infinite love; dwarf their souls so that they can be respectable citizens instead of saints— but make them fit!

The moving picture accompanying the lecture gave an interesting slant on the theory of success. There were two shoes shown: one of a discouraged bum, and the other of a successful business man, looking smart but not very Christian. The dialogue informed us that the one had the "right" childhood, the other did not. Without going into what constituted the "right" childhood, we'd like to pose the question of whether it is guaranteed to produce saints as well as executives.

Security and Childhood

It may appear that I am forcibly attempting to admit a lot of "ultimates" into a harmless discussion of child care that never meant to get involved in "deep" things. But our pediatrician could not leave out ultimates from his lecture for the simple reason *that they are there*. And failure to talk about them does not mean they do not exist. The pediatrician maintained that the child—right from infancy—should be made to feel secure, even though (and here, whether he wanted to or not, he is discussing an ultimate thing) there is no reason to feel secure. Of course, this amounts to kidding ourselves, and deceiving our children. "Feel secure even though there's no reason to be." What happens when the child, after a few years of "feeling secure," finds there is no prop behind him? Won't he begin to feel very insecure, to say nothing of his obvious mental confusion? If he is at all intelligent, he will want the answers. "Feel secure!"

How can we educate a child properly if we don't know the truth ourselves? There is an answer to this question of security. As Christians we can feel secure because we are secure. Before there was a human father to make his child feel secure, there was the paternity of God. And before the first mother made her child content in her arms, there was God Who gave His tenderness. "Can a woman forget her infant, so as not to have pity on the son of her womb? And even if she should forget, yet will not I forget thee." That is the reason we have for making our children feel secure. The providence of God is their security. And children are secure with their parents because the parents are secure with God.

Too often there are women who can forget their children. The doctor who gave this lecture is entrusted with the care of these since he is on the staff of a hospital for abandoned and neglected babies. What is his, and our, answer to these children? How can we make them feel secure unless we act with the memory of the words of God: "And even if she should forget, yet will not I forget thee." One begins to realize this if one holds an unattractive, smelly, half-witted, abandoned baby in one's arms. There is only one answer. "Yea, the very hairs of your head are numbered." And one can go on to raise that baby in security and love only if one has faith in God.

We should like to note here that we agree with the pediatrician if he meant that modern society can't offer security. It can't. And since he is fitting the child into modern society, he can't promise security. But then why expect that mental health will be produced by ignoring facts? And why fit the child into something that will not benefit him? Why not change society to fit his normal mental and moral development?

The Child's Place in the Scheme of Things

The movie we saw opened with the scene of a man and his wife walking into their child specialist's office. They are obviously all in a dither, exceedingly harassed because they think their two-year-old girl is a problem child. (Nature has a way of solving such minor problems. In the normal course of events, if the parents were having another baby by the time little Sandra was two, they would have something else to worry about, and Sandra, on her part, would have the benefit of a *family*, instead of becoming the ever-enlarging angle of a triangle.) The doctor reassures the parents that they have done a good job so far, that most important of all they *wanted* the child. Now we agree that it is an important thing both for the child and the parents that they want the child, but we wonder on whose terms they are supposed to want him. It is only too easy to see an implication that if the child is *planned for*, according to paternal designs, he is wanted. For the Christian parent, the child's being wanted has a deeper meaning. It means that he is *willed by God.*

It is rather strange that before the child is born, or even conceived, the parents have designed the whole thing coolly and with detachment; now that the child is here, he is often the center of the universe. Their life moves around him, he is all absorbing. This may seem good on the surface (and it is good only on the surface, for basically their self-centered lives have not changed) that the parents should be willing to make sacrifices for the child. But sacrifices can be selfish as well as selfless. (Just as a child's being *wanted* is not always good. C.S. Lewis in *The Great Divorce* gives an example of a mother who wanted her son so much that she wanted him in hell with her.) It is not a good love that gives a child a false adoration. For it is no compliment to the child to make him a tin god when he is a Son of God. And truly that is what the child becomes at Baptism. He enters the Royal Family of Christ and the saints.

And that is my complaint: not that children are given too much esteem, but that they are not given esteem enough. This may seem odd when I have already mentioned the super-abundancy of child psychology books, and the great interest in child development. What I mean to say is that children deserve a deeper attention, more awesome and filled with reverence. I think that it was Maurice Zundel who said that every mother has the right to think her baby is the most wonderful baby in the world, because there is only the One Baby. It is because of the coming of Christ that a child should be regarded with intense wonder and admiration. For Christ forever gave the child his title of dignity: *of such is the kingdom of Heaven.* It is a thing to thank God for. Babies are not given to us just for their sentimental value, or because they are fun to play with. They are a lasting reminder from God that unless we become as little children we shall not enter heaven. That is why we can become bad so easily, sophisticated and hardened to the grace of God, if we don't have children around to keep us *little* and simple.

This, then, is the child's place in the scheme of things. It does not mean that just because the child has "supernatural superiority" or "heavenly priority" (if we can call it that) that he is to rule the home. Like Christ, the child is intended to be subject to his parents, to be trained by their love and wisdom and example, and thus himself advance in "wisdom and age and grace with God and man." With man, too, for the child must be trained to develop his natural talents, to learn the dignity of work, and to find his place in society. I mean in a natural, organic society. There is certainly no compulsion to make him fit into a society foreign to his nature.

The Nature of the Child

This brings us to the consideration of the nature of the child. Child psychology says: "We must not make the child conform to adult standards of truth, generosity and goodness."

Now is the child a different species from man? Or is it not true that his nature is the same, but that his potentialities are undeveloped, his capacities unfulfilled? Indeed Saint Paul said: "When I was a child, I spoke as a child, I understood as a child, I thought as a child. But when I became a man, I put away the things of a child." Play is a child's business; it is not man's. A child works in order to learn; a man works in order to earn his living by serving his fellow man. A child's manner, his conduct and approach to things are different from an adult's.

I walked into a settlement house for the first time. Right away a little girl came up to me and said, "We are playing house and you can be the mother." The others agreed. That was that. I was the mother. "When I was a child I thought as a child..."

But this is not to say that the child's nature is essentially different, nor that his ultimate food is not the same, as man's. Nor is it to say that "standards of truth, generosity, etc." are exclusively adult standards. If we say that, we are in danger of implying that these and other moral principles are simply the mores of our society, and not a part of the basic moral law. The Church wisely sets the age of seven years as the general age for the attainment of the use of reason, and for the knowledge of the difference between right and wrong. This carries with it the understanding that even before the age of seven, the child is to be trained according to those principles of morality whose rightness he himself will assent to when he does reach the age of reason. Really, when we break down this contention of so-called "adult standards" versus "natural moral law known to every normal human being," we come to this conclusion: either we train our children according to the nature God has given them with a realization of their consequent moral responsibility, or we train them according to rules super-imposed on their nature by the particular customs of the day. If this latter is true, child psychology is ever-changing. And certainly there is no point in training children according to adult standards if these so fluctuate that the child, even by growing fast, could not keep up with them!

Modern child psychology at the same time over-rates

and under-rates the child. And we Catholics can fall very easily into the same fault by not perceiving the root error. We find standards of truth and goodness unnatural to the child if we fail to see the natural law operating in him, and *especially* if we fail to take into account the perfection of soul to which he is called as a Christian. We do not expect the child to have the wisdom of St. Thomas, the love of St. Teresa or the zeal of St. Francis Xavier, but we should expect to foster the development of these virtues (according to personal capacity) for the moral and spiritual growth that should come to normal maturity. We have no right to under-rate the child.

At the same time we have no right to over-estimate him. We do this if we hold that his training can be accomplished without external discipline. We thus forget about original sin and its consequences. Our pediatrician said, "Discipline from within is the best kind." Granted, but let us not forget the "evil from within" left by original sin. And let us remember that we have to curb and correct certain tendencies of the child. Let us not over-rate his goodness.

Christian child psychology is never divorced from revelation. It remembers the supernatural destiny of the child, and the fall of man; two gigantic realities; the soul restless until it rests in God—and the pull of evil. Remembering these, it can never accede to a naturalistic child psychology, no matter how brilliant and valuable it appears.

Stealing is a moral problem, not just a bad habit like nailbiting. (And that is what Catholic social workers and psychologists find themselves saying under the influence of an "understanding way of dealing with the child's problems.") Masturbation is a moral problem, not a "normal stage of sexual development."

We have a grave obligation to children in whatever position we deal with them—whether we are their parents, or social workers, or teachers, or doctors. In a way those are terrible words of Our Lord's which He uttered after He told us to permit the little ones to come to Him. He said, "And forbid them not." We have to examine our consciences on that to see whether we pay more attention to the cavities in their teeth than to the weaknesses of their souls, to their physical growth than to their growth in holiness, to their social acceptability than to their status as children of God. There are more ways of forbidding children to go to Him than by ordering churches to be closed down and by teaching children to hate Him. Just because we don't worship the devil, it doesn't mean that we worship God. We can *forbid them* by ignoring God, by just never bothering the children with Him, or by raising the children in complete oblivion of their moral and religious obligations. We can *forbid them* by filling the children "with the cares and pleasures and riches of this life," so that His seed never takes root in their hearts. And we *forbid them* to go to God, if we raise our children according to a child psychology that does not have the impetus of supernatural love.

Train the Child in Holiness

I was in church one day when a little boy about five or six walked in, came up to me and said, "When is God coming out? I want so much to see Him." We had quite a conversation. But I think what I told him made little impression, for after he left me I noticed him standing still *watching all the doors!* The point is, the little boy might have had a very erroneous idea of how God is coming, but he had gotten one extremely important thing. Someone had given him the idea that *God is good to see.*

If we train our children to realize why they are here and

to Whom they are going, we have done a great deal. If we give them an ardent longing for God, then we are one step toward being the parents of saints.

As a social worker I visited Catholic foster homes, and it was apparent that where many of the exceedingly small children baffled me with their knowledge of radios, record-players, and the mechanics of a car, a great many did not know their prayers. Either the foster parents were not sufficiently interested in the child's religious training, or (and I feel that this was often the case) they felt that the child was too young for religion.

Perhaps he was too young for formal prayers, but that is not the point. The child should grow up with God, just the way he grows up hearing about his grandmother, without understanding exactly the relationship, but knowing that she is very important. Children will know where God fits in if their parents live and act with the conviction that He is the center of their lives.

There was one foster mother who delighted me. She spoke to the three-year-old twins in a marvellous mixture of Irish brogue and "baby talk." When I asked if they knew their prayers, she replied, "Oh, yes. When they go to bed they say "Good-night, Goddie. Good night, Holy Mary.'"

When I was a child, I prayed as a child...

Then there is Michael, who, because his parents lived in the country several miles from church was taken to Sunday Mass, starting when he was only a few months old. When he had just begun to talk, one Sunday, at the Elevation of the Host, he exclaimed, "Pretty."

"Out of the mouths of infants and sucklings, Thou has perfected praise."

Progressive's Plaint

I am seven.
People say, "how sweet!"
I'm dressed so well—
I'm warm, my feet
Have rubbers. You can tell
someone takes care of me.

I am seven.
I'm always clean. You see
I've no kid brother to start a fray,
No little sisters to play with me.
And yet, how hard for one I pray!

I am seven.
But I'm so old.
I've food and clothes and shelter.
Shots for pox, diptheria, TB, cold,
Send my germs a-helter skelter.
I'm smart in school. My IQ's high.
So, why? Why so old and bitter?
My folks "stay young," while I
Am reared each day by a different sitter!

MARRIAGE FOR KEEPS

ED WILLOCK

There's a difference between being married and being an expert on marriage. There's a difference between having a group of letters after your name and a group of children at your heels. I'm married, with a group of children. I'm not an expert with a Ph.D. Consequently, in writing about marriage I'll not approach it as a subject, but as an experience.

Along with that explanation of the perspective I intend to take, I should add that I am no past-master. My children are not grown up, they are babies and the oldest is eight. We don't know what it would be like to be without an infant in the house. My writing room is not an ivory tower but a kitchen table.

So, there you are. When I speak about children, I'm talking about Mike, Paul, Elizabeth, Ann, Marie, Peter and Clare. Mike breaks windows and says prayers very well. Paul is always smiling, even while he's letting the air out of our neighbor's tires. Ann has the most beautiful eyes for an eight-year-old I have ever seen, but the school examiner tells us she needs glasses. Marie is as shy and as curious as a kitten. She has cheeks like an apple and an appetite like a truck driver. Peter's just beginning to walk and he looks like Dopey the Dwarf. Clare is the center of attention in her bassinet. Tack their pictures on a wall against a background of diapers, milk bills, broken toys, worn-out shoes, outgrown overalls, jam-stained doorknobs, broken glass and complaints from the neighbors, and you begin to see marriage as I see it.

But that's only part of the picture. To see the rest, you must see Elizabeth preparing for her bath in the evening; two feet tall and as formidable as Gibraltar. Just to look at her cherubic countenance after we have flushed off a few inches of topsoil subtracted from the back yard, gives a father a feeling of security. Her smile removes any doubt you might have about the bountiful providence of God. And the evening prayers (in spite of the fact that Ann shows off her facility with words and Elizabeth falls asleep) binds every thread of the day together into a pattern of marriage that is convincing. It's here to stay and it's for keeps. It's a way to spend a life. It's a way to God that's heaven all along the route.

That will give you an idea of the way I tackle marriage, but I'm not speaking only for myself. I didn't invent marriage. It has been with us a long time. I see my family as one unit among millions of families. I see it as a long chain of wedding rings extending back through generations, and this tradition goes back to a table at which Christ sat. There was a wedding banquet and the wine ran out. He changed the water into wine. By His presence there, His act of divine generosity and His sanctification of marriage, He has made the water of marriage into sacramental wine.

Adventure with Christ

Christian marriage is like nothing else, least of all like that caricature of marriage—the typical modern thing (which is a kind of legal cohabitation). It isn't a love song sung with "a girl for you and a boy for me but heaven help us from having three." It isn't two people making the best of an uncomfortable situation. It is an adventure with Christ.

The Pre-Marital Jitters

Along about the last month before the knot is tied, the average fellow begins to bite his finger nails. The girl has taken over and she's in a sweet swoon about the details. The fellow finds himself in a rapidly moving caravan, dashing by jewelry counters, clothes dummys, flats-to-rent ads, consultation of the bank book, furniture stores, draperies, best man, bridesmaid, and all the little details that the girl sees with uncanny intuition. Looming before him is *one* thing, MARRIED LIFE. It's a big thing! What will it be like? Never

TOO LITTLE AND TOO LATE
Planning parents can hardly hope,
　　With two or three but seldom more,
To match a Catherine of Sien'
　　The last but one of twenty-four.

mind about details, look at this big, strange unknown!

Most fellows go through that and so did I. With some very tidy arithmetic I had concluded that we could live as cheaply as one and a half. I had a steady job, as jobs go. We could afford my staying away from work a week, have an inexpensive honeymoon, and then get by on bread and water until the first payday. Of course, we could have grown old apart, instead of together, as so many couples do, waiting until we could *afford* it. "Not for us" said we, and it was clinched!

Marriage was a few weeks away. We hadn't found a place to live. Dorothy lived in one town and I in another. We had decided to set up house in my town. But, as I say, flats (at the rent we could afford) were scarce.

The day I'm describing had been pretty rough. I operated a machine in a small plant. That day, the machine was balky and the stock was bad. I fretted and fumed, my feet itching to be pounding around town, looking for a flat. This one, gnawing desire being frustrated, discolored my entire picture of the future. I went home on the subway in a blue funk. My mother detected the mood as I played golf with my peas at the supper table. So I put it up to her. "Listen, Mom, we've got plenty of room here. Why can't Dot and I move in here after we're married and then we can take our time looking for a flat."

I should have known better! My mother was always a lady for calling a spade a spade (and still is, for that matter). I wouldn't have missed it for the world! Her exact words I don't remember, but they went something like this:

Mom's Sermon

"Listen here, Sonny. I prepared you for Baptism about twenty-three years ago. I nursed you, bundled you up and put your booties on. After that, when you were seven, I tucked in your shirt and brushed down your cowlick when you went to receive your First Communion. At Confirmation you were twelve, and still helpless. I fixed your necktie, tucked in your shirt and sent you off. But (and here she laid it on) if you think for one minute that Mama is going to lead you down the aisle for matrimony and home again, you don't know your mother! Matrimony is for men and women, not for children. If you can't handle this problem on your own, probably the simplest problem you'll ever face as a couple, then you may be old enough to marry, but you're not a man!"

In retrospect, her speech added up to this:

A family needs a head and God designed the man for that role. By nature, the man is aggressive and independent. He works best in the open, free, with liberty to make choices of direction. The woman, on the other hand, achieves her freedom within limits. No matter how valiant she may be, she likes the role of a help-mate to a man of whom she is proud. (A simple little picture that illustrates this point is the fact that in the outdoors, on the plains, in the woods, or behind a plow, a man who is a man, is at home. In such a picture, the woman is dwarfed beside him. As a matter of fact, any woman who does look at home in the great outdoors isn't very feminine. She's likely to have a rasping voice and a horsey look. Just move the couple into a living room and the woman grows in stature. The enclosure reflects her importance.)

Men in our time have not been taking this headship. God forbid that we should return to the tyranny of the Bible-thumping patriarch, but the pendulum is now way over in the other direction. All around us we have seen the way in which men have allowed the brutality of masculine affairs to invade and desecrate the personal environs which the women hold dear.

Wars, the work of men, have ripped the families and slain the children. The economic processes designed by men have depersonalized the worker, prescribed the number of children and turned men into irresponsible paychecks. The neuroses which characterize our times are the result of this assault upon the heart and sensibilities of society. The women, because of their capacity for generous compassion and the sensitivity that such warmheartedness engenders, have borne the brunt of this injustice. The intimate personal concern which it is a woman's glory to give, has been disregarded in the masculine madness of money-making, empire-building and forensic debate.

Women Prefer Marriage

Because of that, women have difficulty trusting the modern man. Most women still prefer marriage, and they would choose marriage if men assured them a dignified and devoted leadership.

Where this lesson particularly applied in my case and in the case of so many fellows today is that we tend to reflect rather than remove the woman's fear of insecurity. Instead of providing a shoulder to be wept upon, too many men go to their mothers, girl friends or wives, looking for a hankie. Yes, a man can be gentle, but he can be a gentle-man. He can softly but firmly lead the way out of difficulties, not capitulate to the fears for the future.

It will always be true in marriage that the greatest giving will be on the part of the wife. Through pregnancy and child raising, she loses the independence which the man continues to retain. If today the woman is reluctant to do this, it is because she does not trust the man to be loving, confident and considerate when she must of necessity depend solely

For carrying social burdens: Individuals are like wheels, they work best in pairs, and when couples work together a very heavy burden can be carried easily.

on him. We confirm this mistrust whenever we hesitate. A good woman is happy to go through torture for her husband as long as his step is firm, his love tender and his faith strong.

When my mother concluded her sermon, I still wasn't convinced. I know better now, but it takes time to grow up. I just grouched away from the table and sat in the parlor glowering at the design in the carpet. The doorbell rang and my mother passed me a telegram. That telegram gave me the deepest, most gratifying bellylaugh that I have ever had. It isn't easy to explain why it tickled me so much or why I still regard it as one of the most provident lessons that God taught me about marriage. All it said was that it was from Dorothy and would I mind changing the date of the wedding because her Aunt Sarah, who lived in Washington, had sprained her leg and would not be able to get there as early as we had hoped.

To get the picture you've got to realize that I was looking at that wedding date with the same awful expectancy of a condemned prisoner marking off his calendar. Then along comes my beloved and kicks that awe-inspiring date into a cocked hat simply because Aunt Sarah had sprained her leg! The scales suddenly fell from my eyes and I discovered with a gasp of joy that a woman always has her lovely finger on somebody's pulse, and that pulse means more to her than the C.I.O., the N.A.M., or the U.N., or all combined, especially more than a paltry wedding date.

Take the man who is directing the setting in place of the central span of the Abraham Lincoln bridge. He gets a call from the construction shack. It's his wife on the phone. "I'm sorry to bother you, dear, but would you mind dropping in to the seven-eleven on the way home and getting some *yellow* paper napkins? It's uncle George's birthday and the frosting on the cake is yellow, and all I have in the house are red ones."

You see, the subtle point of the thing is that the man considers these things *petty*—that is, unless he is the one about whom the fuss is being made. You will never really appreciate a woman unless you have seen her at the end of a day of moving into a new flat, the furniture in disarray, the children bedded in make-shift bunks, quietly putting up the nicely ironed curtains. The mere male dwindles in stature as the woman unobtrusively proves that the dignity of the human soul transcends time and circumstance. It is no wonder that God entrusted His Divine Son as a gentle Babe to the warm, confident love of a valiant woman.

Consideration and Acquiescence

A fellow and girl have to be equipped with a great deal more than mutual infatuation if they hope to survive the difficulties of marriage. During the course of married life I have picked up a working set of principles that help to make for compatibility between the sexes.

To begin with, it is not an easy thing for a man and woman to get along together. I stress this point especially for young lovers who have not yet had a real spat. If there comes a time or occasion when you would be delighted to subject your mate to some form of mayhem, do not consider yourself peculiar. Resist the urge to inflict injury, by all means, but do not for a moment conclude that your marriage is shattered or that love has fled. Saint Paul said that marriage is a great mystery. Every husband and wife has learned that it is a mystery for which there is no solution except love.

The family relationship is a dynamic one. By that I mean that it is a living, moving, maturing relationship. It is not static. It is not the relation between a nut and a bolt, or between a set of gears. The man and woman must become one flesh. Their two lives must fuse together and yet remain vital. The man is not consumed by the woman, nor is she consumed by the man. They must be joined together without any loss of personality. In fact, when a marriage is successful, the personality of both husband and wife becomes more mature, more vital. The man becomes more manly, and the woman becomes more feminine.

Attract and Repel

To make this possible, the two sexes must not only attract one another, but they must also repel one another. This may sound like a contradiction, but it can easily be demonstrated. It is normal, for example, for a man to be attracted to a woman, but it is equally normal for him to be repelled by femininity. No normal man would want to live in a beribboned and scented boudoir. On the other hand, it is normal for a woman to love a man; it is equally normal for her to be repelled by masculinity. No normal woman would like the loud talk, rough comradeship and bare decoration of a barracks or clubroom. The point to be stressed is that a man may love a woman but he hates to be womanly. A woman may love a man but she has no desires to be manly.

The love, then, that should exist between husband and wife can be expected to have the qualities of reverence and respect. In other words, when a husband loves his wife, he must love her because she is a woman and love her as a woman should be loved. He cannot love her as a pal and treat her like one of his football chums. The wife must love her husband because he is a man, and love him as a man should be loved. She must not treat him like a child or regard him as a sorority sister.

In this way, we respect the mystery of marriage. The man will never thoroughly understand the woman and usually admits it. The woman will never thoroughly understand the man, but will seldom admit it. Because of this mystery, the love of a man for a woman has a special character that makes it different from the love of a woman for a man. The nearest we can come to defining this difference is to say that the love of the man must be *considerate* and the love of the woman must be *acquiescent*.

Late for Supper

I could take a few cases from my own experience to show you what I mean by consideration and acquiescence. Suppose I were to work late at the office. As I approach the house after getting off the bus, I try to phrase my excuse in advance so as to placate my wife's very understandable ire at having "spoiled" her dinner. In my mind, the whole excuse boils down to the fact that I just *had* to work late. That's all there is to it! I had to work late. So when I open the door and behold the frown, I say, "I'm awfully sorry, dear, for being late, but I just *had* to work late!" The thunder cloud is not so easily dispelled. But, after all, I *did have to* work late, didn't I?

Before abstracting any lesson from this, let's consider the

opposite situation; when I get home on time and the wife doesn't have the supper ready. Dorothy immediately goes into a lengthy and elaborate explanation: "You see, dear, Mrs. O'Connor called me over to meet Abigail Updyke, who is engaged to Mrs. O'Connor's son. You can imagine my surprise when I discovered that Abigail went to school with Daphne Hothouse. You know Daphne, she was at our wedding—wore a silk taffeta skirt with a belt in the back—Well, you see, Mrs. O'Connor was awfully anxious to make Abigail feel at ease and she was delighted to discover that I have something in common with her—So, you see, one thing led to another..."

This explanation cannot be stemmed. It continues through supper and beyond. Finally, just before going to sleep, my wife breaks into tears, "You simply won't forgive me for not having your dinner ready, will you?" Of course, I have already repeated at fifteen minute intervals for the past four hours, "That's perfectly all right, dear, don't let it bother you one little bit." Naturally, near the end, my words of forgiveness had a slight note of "For Heaven's sakes, *forget it*, will ya!"

I don't intend to pass out a formula for handling such situations as these. My intention is only to demonstrate what I mean by consideration and acquiescence. Please notice that the husband's crisp and precise explanation would have been quickly accepted by another man and the wife's lengthy and elaborate excuse would have met the approval of another woman. In the second case (where the wife makes the excuse), the husband's consideration for the feminine nature of the wife could make the whole thing come off very neatly. He should come to expect lengthy excuses (for that's a woman's way). If, for example, he showed a *certain amount of enthusiasm* for his wife's story (which she is elaborating to take his attention away from her negligence), the first thing you know is that the entire attention would be centered on the story and the late supper would be forgotten.

In the first case, if the wife were to acquiesce to the masculine habit of crisp explanations, and *accept it as a precise statement of fact*, everything would be fine. She needs merely say, "Of course, dear, you had to work late, that can't be helped."

Consideration is an active, aggressive virtue. Acquiescence is a passive, docile virtue. The husband has to summon up his enthusiasm for his wife's lengthy story. The wife has to quiet and pacify her anger at his being late, and also squelch her curiosity for details.

Another example that illustrates consideration and acquiescence is the formality of a man's opening a door for a lady. Picture a couple, arm-in-arm, approaching a closed door. For the entire formality to come off gracefully, the girl must *step back* and the fellow must *step forward*. If the fellow fails to step forward, the girl feels that she has been ill-treated. If, on the other hand the girl fails to step back, the man must either roughly push her aside or else follow her shamefacedly through the doorway. The same kind of consideration and acquiescence are necessary in every intersexual act.

Men Must Lead

Why should this be so? Human experience throughout the ages prescribes that in every joint enterprise of men and women, the man must lead. It would be foolish to defend this male leadership here, because the defense lies with those who doubt it or who can produce a plausible alternative. As individuals, men and women have been endowed by God with an equality in dignity and potential. They do not, however, have the same function to fill in society. It is merely in this role, when their functions are wed to conceive a joint enterprise, that the leadership falls to the man. It is only when men exploit their leadership by active brutality or passive weakness that women refuse to accept the supporting role. Today is just such an era of brutality and weakness. Consequently, there has been a concerted endeavor on the part of women to throw off a yoke that robs them of their dignity. If it is true (and history proves it so) that a woman gains full stature and great dignity beside a virtuous and virile husband, it is equally true that a weak man will have an even more debilitating effect upon his wife.

Human nature does not change, however. If it is true that the men of our generation exhibit a gross brutality in their war and a shameful weakness in their peace, failure on the part of women to acquiesce will do nothing more than aggravate the situation. The wife who refuses to accept the dignity of a supporting role forces her husband to be either brutal or weak. There is no alternative to mutual harmony, and the requirement will always be that the man be eternally considerate of the sensitive nature of the woman and the woman acquiesce to the active aggressiveness of her husband. Sacrifice and great charity is needed in either case.

The Eternal Triangle

I suppose any fellow or girl who ever paused to consider the privilege of being married and of accepting its responsibilities has asked himself if he were worthy or adequate. At one time I thought that I was a bad risk. Suddenly my marrying Dot seemed like a dirty trick on her. My health was not too good. I had a chronic ailment as the result of an early football injury. I'm no genius, especially at making money. Along with that, I have certain principles that I wouldn't violate for any paycheck, a resolve that had made me disliked by more than one boss.

Without being morbid, and just being honest with my-self, I had to admit I was a bad marital risk. Yet I marshalled up the courage to take the plunge, and I have weathered other periods of misgivings which persist to the present day. The key to the riddle is my faith.

Any parent who has ever taken his new baby in his arms and looked at it has had an experience that should have touched his head as well as his heart. No one could believe for a moment, unless he were a presumptuous fool, that this unbelievably wonderful creature, so perfect and brand new, could be an effect of which he and his wife were the sole and simple cause. Could either of you, who hardly know how to care for this creature, who fumble with many thumbs to sustain it, be so foolish as to suppose this child is wholly *yours*? The bare minimum of humility demands a "No!"

This moment can be priceless. It is easy to see a great mystery here. There is a special grace from God that comes with the first visible fruit of matrimony. You suddenly see yourselves as participators in a tremendous drama in which the elements are real and the stake is life. Your part is a great privilege, but a simple task. God has fashioned a body and a soul. You had a part in it, but how little a part, considering this wonderful, tangible, vital infant. With this there would come an awful awareness of the presence of God. This God, Who can in His perfection transcend all things, deigns to become an intimate of our home. His presence here is warm with life. Our babies grow mysteriously; we merely feed and wash them. Then come words and ideas. A new will exerts itself against the bars of the crib. A new consciousness watches the visitor and recognizes the parent. A new personality makes its mark on the high chair and eventually on the world.

Three Providers

You see yourself working along with God. He has enlisted your aid, not you His. He has made you His agent. It
is His plan, His scheme of things, His harvest. You are in
attendance, removing the obstacles to His workings. It is in
the light of this that the idea of being a bad risk is defeated.

For who *is* a good risk? In what way does a million dollars, bountiful health, or human genius guarantee a successful marriage? Are these safeguards against conflicting wills,
sickness or poverty? Not at all! The things that make for
happy marriages, as anyone who is happily married can tes-
tify, are intangible things that moths do not consume nor
with which thieves abscond. In fact, it is money and the
power it gives, it is human genius with its ugly pride, and it
is the constant concern about opinions and possessions, to
which divorces attribute their failure.

Trust in God not only is a guarantee of our needs, as
Christ promised it would be, but it also disposes our minds
and wills to bear with the difficulties of conflicting wills.
God's spiritual gifts of mutual charity and trust are far more
precious and indispensable than His bounty in providing
bread.

Knowing this, I told my wife right at the beginning that
there was only one reason why she should trust me in spite
of my obvious failings. That reason was that I trusted God.
The strength of our family would not depend upon Daddy's
right arm, his foresight, his intrepid character, but rather
upon the infinite mercy of God, Who is more concerned for
our good than we are, and far more capable of providing for
it. There are three providers in our house, Christ and His
two agents, my wife and me.

Fidelity in Marriage

The faithfulness of partners in marriage is a thing seldom discussed. Those who are unfaithful usually try to keep their infidelity a secret, and those who are not, consider infidelity as something "nice people don't do." This secretive attitude might be appropriate were it not for the fact that infidelity is no longer a rare and isolated event, but rather a social epidemic. Conversations in shops, club rooms, and offices would be enough to indicate its prevalence, but in addition we have the infidelity of pre-marital sex-relations, and the infidelity of tandem remarriages.

To regard unfaithfulness as the isolated and strictly personal affair of the parties concerned is to overlook the entire significance of human contract. The bond which unites men harmoniously in society is trust in a common God, and trust in one another. All human relations depend for their proper resolution on an exchange of trust and confidence. At the root of each social contract, whether between co-partners in business or between nations, lies the most sacred, most selfless, and most intimate of all contracts—marriage. Nowhere, apart from the strict profession of religious life, do you find a greater relinquishing of human privilege for the sake of a common goal than in marriage.

The ultimate infidelity, divorce, strikes a murderous blow at the innocent children who cannot help but be left with a wound that grows fetid with mistrust and cynicism. As the children grow, they carry a wariness into their relations with others. The divorce society shies away from all commitments and violates every contract. When this paranoia becomes political, you have something like Soviet Russia and Nazi Germany—mistrust and persecution manias hover like ghosts over the conference table, and wars are waged in the name of imaginary injustices.

From each family flows a tiny spring that empties into the moral reservoir of society. Here at its source the waters are either purified or polluted. When the pollution has reached the reservoir, the moral health of every social institution is jeopardized.

Chastity—The Guardian

Standing watch over this entire process of human intercourse is the virtue of chastity. This picture of guardianship would be ludicrous were we to portray chastity in the role assigned her by the prude or the libertine. It is to the advantage of those who reap personal or corporate profit from moral degeneracy to reduce chastity to the level of a cartoonist's old maid whose only claim to fame is a record of "no hits, no runs, no errors." If we look at the thing boldly, however, and realize that the fate of nations depends upon the inviolability of contracts, and that the marriage contract is the keystone in the contractual arch, and that chastity is the guardian of the marital act, then we must conceive of a virtue—of an adequacy—that demands the heroic.

Chastity fills this role and fills it well. It is in the pure splendor of new love that chastity takes root in marriage, when the young lovers regard their union as inviolate. Their ardor would abhor nothing as much as infidelity. This vital tree is cultivated through sickness, trials and failures, and bears fruit and casts seeds as their children are betrothed and marry. There is no greater tribute of man to man than this concentration of love on one person undeterred. Infidelity is the love-tragedy, the ultimate betrayal of every human confidence.

Immodesty—The Enemy

The alarming thing about infidelity is its ability to grow

without studied malice. Those who betray their wives or husbands usually do not violate their vow in hatred, but in despair. Their passions refuse to be subservient to their love. Consequently, the enemy to be sought out and destroyed is not infidelity or divorce, but the virus which breaks down resistance. The name of the virus is immodesty.

When we concentrate upon immodesty our inquiry covers a broader social field. The provocations to lust are not limited to those areas where lust can be satisfied. The unhappy fact is that very chaste women frequently dress as though they were not. The most faithful wives often dress as though they were advertisements for infidelity. Thus the theatre and movies, the advertisements and novels, the styles and postures, spread their propaganda for lust into every home, and those who feel the least vulnerable may be the first to become infected.

The most striking evidence for this is the impossibility of finding today a living symbol for the chaste spouse, the valiant woman, yet within a hundred yards of wherever you may be, you can find in print or in the flesh, a symbol of female prostitution. It was just such a lack of dignified symbol that recently led a young Jewish psychologist to the discovery of the Blessed Virgin Mary.

In her, he saw woman glorified, fruitful, valiant and inviolate. In her, he saw a modesty that was not a posture, but an exterior radiance that clothed her dynamic vitality. Summed up in all the veneration extended to Mary throughout the ages, he saw the challenge to today's glorification of the street walker. He concluded as I have concluded, that the salvation of human fidelity and the sacredness of contracts ultimately depends upon the veneration of womanhood glorified. Fortunately for us, Christ has given us not merely a symbol but a mother of flesh and blood who stands through time and eternity as the prototype of humanity redeemed, invulnerable to sin, triumphant over temptation, free from treachery.

The Children—Focus of Family Concern

George Bernard Shaw once said that if a man lived three hundred years he would know everything. G.K. Chesterton answered, "Yes, and if Shaw lived three hundred years, he would be a Catholic." The point Shaw had in mind when he made the crack was that history tends to repeat itself. Mankind is always sitting in the pasture of history, rechewing its own cud. In any three-hundred-year period, all theories and revolutions prove themselves either true or untrue, either sane or insane. What Chesterton had in mind was that any man who saw his own lifespan within a perspective of three hundred years would see the logic of Christianity and the need of a Church to perpetuate that logic through history.

To understand marriage we must also regard it from a perspective that embraces a number of generations, otherwise we do not see it *wholly.* Matrimony is a love affair, but it is a love affair in which many more than two people take part. Two is company, but it takes at least three to make a family.

Suppose, for instance, that we look at marriage according to the current mores, what do we see? We see two people in love. They are young and at the height of their idealism and vigor. They marry. The first few months are preoccupied with mutual adoration. Reasonably and observably this can't go on forever. When the fever-heat of the honeymoon has cooled, what is left? They usually try to bank the fire and, while reducing its intensity, attempt to extend its quiet warmth throughout the years. As time goes on, and the lovers grow in age, their attempts at maintaining their love become frantic and all-absorbing. In their narrow scheme of things the climax has passed and all that is left is a prolonged and inevitable anti-climax. They proceed from youth to old age, and finally to the grave. Their love story is more tragic than that of Romeo and Juliet. It is suicidal, but a suicide extended over many dull years, rather than over a few dramatic moments.

Marriage and Life

But contrasted with this concept of marriage, let's try to see it in the perspective of generations. Two people meet, each of them an heir to a valuable heritage. They bring to the altar an inheritance of culture, of wisdom and of faith. Their ancestors suffered, died, endured sea voyages, imprisonment, preserving this treasure which the two lovers offer one another when they plight their troth. In their marital embrace they generate the seed of a new generation who will take these historic gifts and weave them together in a new pattern—a new way of life. The process of events is no longer tragic as the lovers grow old they see their early vigor transplanted in their children. The children become adept at using the cherished culture, wisdom and faith.

This glorious tradition blossoms anew within the family. The parents are unaware of their declining years and passing youth because they are too engrossed, cultivating a new and more wonderful life in their children.

Without this conception of marriage as a vehicle for extending a life of culture, wisdom and faith throughout the years, the entire adventure and the very reason for marriage is lost. Without it, marriage is a flash in the pan, a glorious sky-rocket that drops in a moment, charred and inert. We cannot, however, maintain this conception of marriage unless we truly cherish the culture, wisdom and faith to which we are heirs. If life for us means no more than the thing that began at our birth and ends with our death, then we, in truth, have no troth to plight. We are asking our beloved to wed tomorrow's cadaver, to share a requiem, to share our grave.

The Christian home is a shrine that glorifies a living culture, wisdom and faith. It is not a museum for the accumulation of outmoded gestures, relics of the past, but a place of new birth. In the children the faith comes to life, taking on new forms, developing unique social patterns.

All the moralizing against birth control is almost always in vain unless this vital conception of marriage is retained. Who would have children if the end of childhood were nothing but a dull wait for death? Who would want children if he had no treasure to offer them? Who would give life unless life had an eternal significance, dating back to Genesis and extending forward to eternal union with God?

In the modern scheme of things the child too often comes as an obstacle to the parents' wallowing in their own childish and selfish indulgences; whereas in the Christian scheme of things the child becomes the focus of family concern, the new messenger, the new apostle, to carry the flame through another generation.

The Christ-life Lived

Realizing this, Dorothy and I are trying to revive the cultural patterns of the past and adapt them to the new generation in which Ann and Marie, Paul and Michael, Elizabeth, Peter and Clare, will live. We want them to know and appreciate the Christian thing as it was appreciated in ages past, as it is understood today by the Catholic natives of Hong Kong, of Czechoslovakia, of Italy. During the weeks before Christmas, the Advent wreath is hung and its candles lighted, while the sole absorption of many neighbors is with Christmas shopping. Christ comes into our house on Christmas Day and the Infant remains with us through the Epiphany. The children learn of the exchange of gifts, the constant beneficence of God. Later we go through Lent. Michael learns a new significance for the bumped head and the scraped shin-bone as he vaguely perceives the positive value of suffering. Easter is a glorious reward for the endurance of fasts and penances, consonant with their age and capacity.

The significance centers, not in pious gestures, but the children are taught the Christ-life lived. Justice and charity in their dealings with playmates. Poverty and ingeniousness in their little arts, such as those exemplified in the carpenter shop at Nazareth.

Slowly they will perceive the vast Christian mission and their part in it, the splendid adventure of restoring to Christ a world that has strayed. Their pettiness will be replaced by a docility to greatness. They will become alarmed at the vacuity of selfishness and let that vacuum be filled with divine purposefulness.

Children mean just that to us. We do not pray and work so that everything will *go* well. Our concern is that everything will *grow* well. Will we try to become better-off for the sake of the children? No! We will try to become better for the sake of the children, because by becoming better we will become closer to God Who is the Source of all good, material and spiritual, and because we have learned that the desire to become better-off is just as likely to exclude children as to include them.

The Will of the Child

The last few paragraphs may be a little top heavy with

the idea of placing traditional burdens on young shoulders. We haven't forgotten that each child has a life of its own to be led. A child never goes according to the book. Each one is unique, and the formula for each one's happiness differs in details from that of the other.

Persons who have no children usually possess dogmatic principles for raising them. It is sheer poetry to envisage children as either saints or devils. Experience proves that each child is a unique combination of conflicting elements. The parent must strive gently to resolve those conflicts, always respecting the delicate instrument with which he works. When a child does something against the wishes of the parent, his motive may be either weakness, love, malice, ignorance, fear or imitation. For example, Mike constantly strays out of the neighborhood. We have had to put the police on his tail at various times. Should this crime be treated as malicious disobedience? No! Mike has a memory that doesn't retain a thing. He proceeds from one wonderful experience to the other. Even on the way to the woodland his anticipation is forgotten in the delight of watching a passing butterfly! Virtue must be made adventurous for Mike or he's not interested.

Marie is sent to the corner store. She returns an hour later with some strange tale and no groceries. Marie is timid and she just waits until the proprietor finds her down below the counter. Paul talks back to his Grandma simply in imitation of the sport he has with the neighbors' teen-age boys. Here and there is malice, unbalanced nature, original sin forcing its way through. Each of the motives must be recognized. Malice is punished. Imitation is channeled. Ignorance is instructed. Fear is dispelled. Weakness is strengthened. Never is the will bent too far, but only slowly and carefully, in keeping with its nature.

Learning from Children

Influence in the home is by no means one-sided. If the family dynamic is working properly while the children are being counselled by the parents as to the ways of adulthood, the parents are being reminded by the youngsters of the virtues of childhood. Any parent who is honest with himself has his tongue in his cheek whenever he says, "I don't know why it is that Junior persists in doing the things I tell him not to do!" At such a time he cannot help but think of his own disobedience and perversity in relation to God. Why do we, the parents, persist in our disobedience to God?

What adult, when talking to a youngster, does not envy his guilelessness and sincerity? His upturned face so open and sincere? Often I have brought worries home only to have them dispelled by the gaiety of the children. Their happy innocence gives us a nostalgia for the innocence of the sons of God. "Unless you become like little children," Christ said, "you will not enter into the Kingdom of Heaven." How fortunate to have the evidences of childhood all around us to pin-prick our sophistications and remind us of our helplessness before God.

Adulthood can become an awfully grim and desperate state unless it is tempered by the sanity of childhood. Yet the homes today are few and far between in which you can find that elusive ingredient. The vogue now is to tolerate the child within an adult milieu. Mother and father keep their world autonomous, limiting the children to playpens. The children are bribed with toys to keep their distance. The tribulations of the child are treated as so many "cases" with the formal competence more becoming to a social worker than a parent. Fortunately with a brood as large as ours, childhood cannot be relegated to an area. It's all over the place. Lonely children sense this and seek out our home as though it were an oasis. In spite of their electric toys and three-shift tri-cycles, they would rather spend their time among our young-sters. In the eyes of the children, it is our brood who are privileged because our home is *for* children, not for grown-ups. In other houses you may find a child, but in our house you can find *childhood*.

Fear and Worry

One experience we had that has done much to relieve us of fears and worries was that which occurred when we were expecting our fourth baby. We were living fairly snugly in a finished attic in a pleasant neighborhood. Things had become somewhat crowded since the time we had moved there as starry-eyed newlyweds. The landlady didn't like our propensity for propagation. She didn't like the wailing and gnashing of teethings, and she also felt that large families reduced the value of real estate; this in spite of the fact that we had painted and decorated the exterior and interior of the house. She had asked us to leave.

We had gone about on Sunday afternoons, scouting the area for vacant flats. If there had been some way by which we could have boiled down our three children into one dog, we might have made the grade with some landlords. With three toddlers, we didn't have the chance of a communist in the N.A.M. (National Association of Manufacturers).

This had not bothered us too much until my wife be-came pregnant. The attendant increased sensitiveness made her more vulnerable to the scathing remarks of the landlady. We were also learning that having a large family so close together shared the same social stigma as chronic drunken-ness or dope-peddling. Our neighbors and relatives com-pounded a hypocritical concern for our plight with an equally obvious unwillingness to assist us in any way. Our spirits were at a low ebb.

At that time I was working as a shipping clerk in a warehouse. We were very busy and overworked. My chronic ailment had become worse. In addition to that, I had been giving all my leisure hours to the preparation of the yet unborn INTEGRITY.

One evening a friend of mine dropped in to mind the children while Dot and I went to see the doctor. He had unpleasant news for us. "It is impossible," he told us, "at this late date to make a hospital appointment for your wife." The hospitals were overcrowded and beds were scarce. The second piece of news was that I had to take a month in bed, or else.

Well, that was the picture when we went home that night. Here were all the circumstances that trembling newlyweds foresee with horror. Sickness, eviction and childbirth, and no money in the bank. The way the thing worked out has only reconfirmed our trust in God and taught us something about the way He acts.

We prayed and asked the prayers of others. We encouraged one another and went ahead with our plans. To my great surprise the company paid my salary for the month of absence. I felt no compunction in accepting it because I had spared no effort in their behalf during the preceding two years. The rest left me free to concentrate on the magazine plans, undisturbed by the urgency that I had felt before. My wife was shunted to another, less expensive doctor who found her a bed in a truly Christian hospital, and her lying-in period was the happiest she had known.

Shortly after my recovery, I came to New York where we were planning to publish the magazine. My associates and I made a novena of prayers, and I placed an advertisement in the newspaper reading, "Undesirable tenant wishes to rent

apartment. Have four children and will probably have more."
There was one answer. A small house, badly in need of repairs, was available in a suburban part of the city. I plastered
up the sagging ceilings, repaired the furnace, and we all moved
in.

Trial and Triumph

In retrospect it is obvious that what we had at first considered to be great troubles, were actually the stepping stones
to great treasures. When we were at what appeared to be the
depth of our miseries, we were in fact on the threshold of a
new adventure. The poets have made much of this universal
experience, phrasing it in such ways as "the darkest hour is
just before the dawn." The Christian can see a more mysterious element and abstract a more profound conclusion.

God desires our faith or complete trust in Him. He per-
mits troubles and fears to arise so as to strengthen our faith,
much as a football coach will drill his squad vigorously so
that their strength will grow. Every ill to which the human is
prone exists singly for the purpose of our placing our trust
in God. We do this by bearing with the suffering but always
with the realization that we will at last be triumphant.

If we reject the trial through timidity, we inevitably reject the triumph and fail to gain the reward. A man who
resorts to dishonesty in order to swing a deal because he
fears that honesty will gain him nothing, by so doing erects
an obstacle between himself and God's providence. A new
baby has often been the occasion for a husband's getting a
promotion and a wife's regaining her health. Yet most people
deny themselves children on the erroneous presumption that
a new baby inevitably means unhappiness. In their denial of
the sacrifice, they turn away from God's bounty. God's concern for them, His desire for their happiness, is continuous

and generous, but they, through timidity, refuse to grasp the cross which will release the treasure.

Trust God–Help Yourself

The enemies of Christianity have always used whatever weapons might be lying around without regard for truth or fair play. The communist weapon is slander. They do not condemn a Christian belief for what it is but try to prove it is something else, less grand, less desirable. Ever since the death of Christ there has been a campaign on foot to deform His simple teachings. One of the most subtle of these lies is the one that makes a trust in God's providence *appear to be* an excuse for sloth and irresponsibility. It is true that a religious man is not money-hungry, nor does he want to get the best of his neighbor in a deal, but it is not true that a trust in God makes him less diligent.

The married man today must trust in God and that implies much more work and greater ingenuity than he would need if he were single, or without faith. Society makes little, if any, provision for the responsibilities of parenthood. The prices of children's clothing, rents, doctors' bills and natal care are all in the luxury bracket. Yet there is no corresponding increase in his income. He must shoulder all the extra burdens that go with sustaining unproductive children, and rather than receiving help, he is considered foolish, ostracized from many areas of the city, charged exorbitant sums for children's clothing, excluded from associations he can no longer afford to belong to, and frequently must work for longer hours at a lower rate of pay.

To do this requires hard work and ingenuity. The father of a normal-sized family must learn to take care of as many of his own needs as possible. He can't afford to be without a set of simple tools and the knowledge of how to use them.

He must be able to make minor electrical, carpentry, plumbing and mechanical repairs. The wife, in turn, must also, in spite of her additional burdens, acquire skills that will lessen the need for calling in experts.

My wife has saved many dollars of doctors' bills by learning to diagnose and treat minor ailments. We have learned the proper procedure in first aid and medical treatments for the innumerable germs and accidents that invade a family. Not long ago, by a simple trip to the distributor's and fifteen minutes with a screwdriver, I saved the cost of a repair bill for my refrigerator. With a pair of hair clippers, I can rival the average barber at giving the boys a haircut. Things have to be really bad before we must resort to doctors' fees and the bills of repair men.

Beyond this there is the need to keep our children entertained as well and with far less money than that expended by our less productive neighbors. We must teach them games and build them toys. The toys must be beyond comparison with the store-gotten fantasies showered on the pampered kid next door. We must instill in our children a sense of leadership so that they will not grow timid under the persecution that nice people dish out to what they so hypocritically term the "underprivileged."

Trust in God implies a mighty diligence and an adventurous ingenuity. Please notice that under the time-honored system of Christian marriage, husbandry and house-wifery are not the moronic vocations that the careerist deceitfully claims they are. A father who places life first, who not only accepts children but really provides for them, is likely to make more decisions in a day than a business executive makes in a month. His life is intensely interesting. There is no time for boredom. He must be a philosopher, a craftsman, a politician, a doctor, a psychologist, an administrator and a poet.

His wife must be a nurse, a teacher, an artist, a hostess and a director of souls. The society of the future is made under the eyes and hands of the mother and father, for after the child leaves the home the fate of society and his role in it has already been decided.

A Family of Families

It is no surprise that today's family has come in for such a beating once you realize that the family spirit is just the opposite to cut-throat competition. No one expects that one of a gang of robbers holding up a bank will stop to pick up a lady's handkerchief or help an old lady across the street with her bundles. For the same reason you can't expect the family spirit to survive in a society where everyone is concerned with *self*-expression, *self*-aggrandizement, and even the religious people solely concerned with *self*-improvement. This is especially true when the idea of self-improvement is divorced from the traditionally Christian notion that the way to self-improvement is self-sacrifice.

Christ told us we must love God and love our neighbor. He did not need to tell us to love ourselves or further our own ambitions. If we really want to be perfect and perfectly happy, we gain this state by seeking the happiness of others and not bothering too much about ourselves.

I have already indicated that this modern self-centeredness makes a unity between the husband and wife thoroughly impossible. The modern man and woman lack the generosity for sacrifice that is required before two bodies and two souls can work in harmony. It is precisely this self-centeredness that the Sacrament of Christian Matrimony was designed by God to erase.

Christian Matrimony provides a God-given grace that sublimates our natures so that the man and wife are enabled to overcome their human selfishness and to become docile to the daily task that lies before them. This grace not only tends to unite man and wife, but it also unites family with family. This is a fact that my wife and I discovered only after many preliminary mistakes.

All by Ourselves

You see, we were a pair of starry-eyed idealists when we walked away from the matrimonial altar, hand-in-hand. I'm not sorry about that. If there is one time when the heart should be filled with daring plans and great adventure, it should be on the day of marriage. Because we were idealists, we knew the scorn which the modern world has for ideals. It isn't the man who can hold an ideal that is admired today, but the man who can swing a deal. Our contemporaries are not interested in prophets but in profits.

Even before we were married, the persons were few and far between who truly *encouraged* us in our hopes. Everyone and his brother, it seems, feels obligated to warn the prospective bride and groom of the precautions that must be taken against disaster, even the "disaster" of having children. Advice for the engaged has the grim quality of modern bookkeeping that fastens its eyes not on success, but upon bankruptcy and resale. After being subject for so long to such wet-blanket counsels, we decided to keep our ideals to ourselves. We were not marrying on speculation, we were playing for keeps. If no one believed this, then we would keep it as our own secret.

As we furnished our home and had our first children, and developed family customs, we kept pretty much to ourselves. We were friendly with our neighbors and relatives, but never intimate. We did not wish to have our ideals challenged. We wanted a Christian family life without having to defend our position at every step.

The time came, however, when we saw that things cannot be handled quite so neatly. An ideal is not a thing that is meant to be hung as an immaculate sword about the fireplace, but a thing to become bloodstained and muddy in battle. The occasion for this lesson was the arrival of our third baby.

At that time we had neither a telephone nor a car. As is inevitable, the first pangs of childbirth came at the cold, unholy hour of 4:00 a.m. I had to fumble into my clothes, run across the street to a neighbor, wake him and beg the use of his phone. I received no response to my calls for a taxi, and had to go to another neighbor for the use of his car. Much to my delight and humiliation, the same neighbors whom I had tried to keep out of my affairs so assiduously, were extremely generous when I asked them to *help* me with my affairs. If I had wished to do so, I could have taken a vacation at that time and left the care of the two children to these friendly women. I did not do this, but I did gain a far more valuable service from them because I learned in an unforgettable way that the family cannot and should not, no matter what its ideals may be, exist for itself, but that it must be part of a community of families.

Neighborliness

The fact that these people, in times of emergency, leaped happily to the aid of a family in need, proved to me that if this same neighborliness were revived as a continuous social attitude, each individual family would have a far greater chance of survival, as well as an opportunity to grow normally.

Having our ideals challenged did us no harm. Most of our neighbors had accepted in varying degrees the sterile and fatal prescription for marriage dispensed by the popular magazines and upheld by popular opinion. They did not regard children as a blessing but as a burden. The women were more intent upon retaining the appearance of youth than gaining the dignity of dedicated motherhood. The husbands were more concerned about making more money, than passing on to their children a spiritual bank account that can never be over-drawn. Making friends with such people meant many an argument, and a certain weariness at defending our principles. But, as I say, it was worth it. We were forced by such intimate contact to re-examine our stand. If we were right, we became more convinced. Where we had become spiritual snobs, we were forced to admit it. Many of the people who would not accept our high ideals practiced a charity in their lives far greater than ours. Some who practiced birth control were more patient with children they had than we were with ours.

We learned about all that despite any difference of religious views or practical policies, God intended that we should *need* one another. We learned that our family was only a small part of a larger and greater family. We became aware in a very practical way of the implication of that magnificent Christian teaching called the Mystical Body of Christ: that all men are part one of the other, and the Head of that Body is Christ.

This was not all we learned. The more we sought to live in charity with our neighbors, the more we observed the universal hunger that people have for the spiritual food the Church dispenses. Sometimes, for example, in the course of an evening's conversation, we would mention a Christian truth that we had come to look upon as commonplace. Our guests would be amazed and ask us to repeat it. They would carry it away as a treasure, and before long they would have

made it as important a part of their lives that we would be
ashamed at having let it become commonplace.

Community and Providence

God makes use of the community as an instrument of
His providence. No family has everything it needs all the
time. Few families have everything they need at any time.
Yet if many families were to add up their needs and possessions in a collective pool, perhaps all of them would be able
to extract all that they needed at a given time. I can hear
harsh words of "communism" in the background, but that is
utter nonsense. Wherever people have lived together in harmony since the beginning of time, there has always been a
spirit of mutual co-operation. It is thoroughly perverse for
any family to be forced to conclude that it is completely
dependent upon its own efforts. Yet this is the spirit of today. So afraid are we to depend upon our neighbors in time
of need that we timidly hoard every penny against such a
day. Private property is a good thing and so is thrift, but if
the emphasis on them is so great that each family becomes
an independent kingdom, then society will destroy itself.

At the present time I am engaged in building a group of
houses in company with thirteen other families. We have
been at it but a short time, but yet long enough to see the
tremendous benefits of neighborly co-operation. First of all,
hardly any of us would have considered the possibility of
owning our own homes, for, since we have large families and
average incomes, we could not possibly afford it. It is yet to
be proved that we can do it or afford to do it in a group, but
we are working as though it were possible. This working
together has given us new assurance and moral courage. We
have helped each other in various ways and will grow in
knowledge of community co-operation. Already men have

learned skills and wives have reconfirmed one another's faith in Christian living. Each family knows that if it suffers it will not suffer alone, and if it prospers, the others will rejoice. We are not competing against one another, but seeking a common goal as a complementary company of neighbors.

Families LIVE Together

The alternative to this is for each family to go ahead, seeking its own, letting the Devil take the hindmost. Yet every family that breaks up, or becomes dependent upon the state for support, threatens the entire society of families. New laws are invoked to meet the breakdown of the family, and these laws limit the liberty of other families as well as condoning the weakness. The fact that most families can no longer own property has caused us to lose a respect for property. This, in turn, causes us to relax our vigilance against the development of a government policy which will eventually make ownership completely impossible. The municipal apartment dwellings are an insult to a free people: concrete birdhouses for government wards so small that there is no room for children. We can neither rant nor fume against this unless we seek the only alternative: free co-operation of families to build houses in spread-out areas, where there will be room for children, shops, vegetable gardens and livestock.

It is very sad that engaged couples and newly-weds when they are young and vigorous cannot be persuaded to join forces with others and do things in a community way. When the third and fourth child come along it is hard then to face the obvious fact, that our urban society does not *want* normal families. They suddenly realize that they must rely on their own efforts at a time when their cares and burdens are greatest.

Thank Heaven, more and more men are buying tools

and meeting at planning sessions. More and more wives are sewing together, shopping together, and minding each other's babies. There is some residual Christian liberty and American independence left so that a welfare state and a communist state will not evolve without our putting up a good fight. Families are coming together, yours and mine, and discovering this splendid thing—a community.

"Yes" to God—"Yes" to Each Other

Not long ago my wife and I had a few moments of peace together. I had arrived home from the office after a day of tiring conferences, capped by the usual hour on the subway. The seven children were having their supper and my wife's hectic day was at its climax. Ann had been told in school that she needed glasses. Marie had pictures to show me which she had painted in kindergarten. Paul was in line for a spanking for having resisted a neighbor's attempts to remove him from his rear bumper. Michael had a cold. Elizabeth had fallen downstairs. Peter's new tooth had blossomed beautifully in the middle of his grin. Clare, too, had a cold.

We organized the rambunctious crew through their supper, washed them up, packaged them in their pajamas and lined them up for prayers. Paul was able to get through the "Hail Mary" without any help. Michael characteristically thanked God and asked God for "food." Elizabeth made the others giggle when she said "blessed is the soup" instead of "blessed is the fruit."

Prayers having been finished, we tucked them in bed. Everything had been tended to except listening to Ann's "reading." God bless you's were exchanged and Dot and I sat down at the kitchen to eat our cooled-off dinner. Surprisingly enough, the children went immediately to sleep. We became suddenly aware of the ticking of the kitchen clock—things were that quiet!

Suddenly a feeling of great peace descended upon us. We lingered over a second cup of tea and began to reminisce. Nine years of married life were behind us. We talked about our various experiences together. I asked Dot which of these experiences struck her as being the happiest. We both knitted our brows and tried to remember. After a while Dot said, "You know, I don't think I was ever more happy with you than I am right at this moment." I had to admit with some surprise that I felt the same way!

Ours, we think, is a successful marriage. How do we account for success when all the trials and troubles we go through are the very things that other people avoid as pitfalls? I suppose that at the root of the happiness is a mystery. Through a process of elimination, we always arrive at the conclusion that it is nothing but God's helping grace. We are living a Sacrament. All the other things that seem to explain our peace in the midst of trouble are more an effect than a cause. Certainly a husband's love matures as he sees his wife constantly attentive to the endless demands of the children, rising in a cold bedroom to early-morning emergencies. His love is no longer a fairy-thing, floating in the mirages of courtship. This is a woman with courage and a capacity for sacrifice. She is no stoic, no creature of iron will and vigorous constitution. She is a woman sensitive to pain, yet beyond pain when someone else needs attention. I have not the slightest doubt that come hell or high water, Dot will be right beside me, doing a masterful job. She may weep, but she will work through her tears and she will smile when a smile is needed.

There is a strength far beyond our own that mans the helm of our family ship. Each joy and sorrow has a place in the divine scheme of things. Take one iota of trouble away, and the balance would be lost, the happiness less poignant, the peace less complete. This is Christian marriage, a star, real, practical, full adventure, a thing of days, nights, years and eternity. The price we pay is merely to reiterate the original vow, "I will," saying over and over again, "Yes" to God and "Yes" to each other.

THE VOCATION OF PARENTS

"MRS. J."

Saint Francis de Sales said, "The purpose of parenthood is to people the earth with adorers of God and to fill heaven with saints." And there it is.

We can base all our ideas on bringing up children on this motive. It is a consideration for every married couple with children, for all souls who hope some day to be parents. There is the whole purpose of parenthood. It follows then that everything we do in relation to our children should have that end in view.

This is the task to which mothers and fathers should be dedicated. How few parents are working toward that end, however! Why are they neglecting to do so? Not out of sheer perverseness, usually, but mainly because ever so many, even Catholics, do not know the purpose of parenthood. As a matter of fact, many Catholics in spite of memorized catechism lessons are hardly aware of the purpose of their own existence: to know God, to love Him, and to serve

Him forever in heaven. And though we may not condone their senseless driftings through life, neither must we hastily condemn them.

Mothers

We know there are mothers today neglecting that goal of parenthood, but not because they are deliberately ignoring it. Rather they are ignorant of it.

But mothers should be told and should be reminded over and over again. And it must be impressed on them that they should give unstintingly all the time and consideration required for the task.

In our day most mothers are not remiss in child care. We cod-liver oil them, feed them, dress them well. We attend to all the rules of hygiene and health. Even the poorest of us give remarkable care to these aspects of child-raising. When I lived in a slum clearance housing project mothers regularly attended classes in "nutrition" and other lectures at the health center. They brought their babies for "shots" for prevention of various diseases; they made use of the variety of medical and dental treatment offered by New York City's free health stations, and its hospitals, clinics and dispensaries. There was a surprising amount of talk among neighbors concerning child care, child education, child psychology.

Yet while we raise strong, sturdy bodies and alert, lively minds, we are apt to leave their souls stunted, warped, left in a foreverness of infancy. Their minds and bodies take up our time and effort. Their souls are tightly closed buds that may never be opened to the light of God and blossom on this earth.

When we once know what parenthood is all about and recognize what is before us, we will learn to love and study our children in a new, bolder, stronger way. We will have willing ears for their childish chatter and we will have more patience and joy with them. Mothers must look on their little ones as souls that belong to God and whom He holds dear. Then we will lift our daily living with the children to a higher level than we might achieve with the most noble of materialistic ideals.

The charge is commonly made that mothers are too "tied down," their existence is too drab, they are shut away from the world. If only we could be shut away from the world! Actually for most of us the truth is that the world is too much with us. We are being suffocated by it.

With radio on from rising till retiring, gab sessions on the telephone, the "dailies," the picture-splattered magazines filling in, in panting sentences, the details omitted on the broadcast bulletins and now in more and more homes, television, too—we are taken up in a whirl by the world. How does a mother manage to keep her nerves calmed, her emotions stable when they are so constantly under attack?

And most of us have a particular weak spot. I'll admit it's politics, the state of the nation and the world that disturbs me. Then I know a woman who gets worked to near hysteria by the radio soapbox serials. After one particularly trying day at the radio, she was in tears when her husband came home from work, and couldn't prepare his supper, she was so broken up over the adventures of Ma-Soap-and-So. And she was not a neurotic, middle-aged woman but a young bride. There are others whose minds are always filled up with the gossips and sins (imaginary or otherwise) of their neighbors and the affairs of their own assorted relatives. There are mothers to whom cleanliness is such a fetish that they are always drawn taut and tense with housecleaning, laundering, and face washing (usually accompanied by slappings and scoldings) their little ones, and are frightfully disturbed over smudges on their scrubbed-down domains.

It does not matter whether we are preoccupied with national affairs, gossip or a shiny floor, the Devil achieves his aim when such things interfere with our home life and our children. It is true that children can "get on your nerves," cause you to blow up, become sharp and short-tempered. But if we find it happening daily and many times a day we ought to search our hearts to see if it is actually the children who are the cause or if their annoyances are only the fuel that sets off a powder keg of nerves and irritation inside us; a powder keg we ourselves filled up with outside misery that should not have been permitted entrance in the first place.

Perhaps it is good for mothers to be "up-to-the-minute," smart, socially active, but first of all they should be *mothers*. If we can't be everything, then let's not put motherhood in last place or out of the running. What our children need are their mothers. So we ought to concentrate on that, living strictly according to our vocation, being worthy of it, seeking to perfect ourselves in it.

Yes, to be a mother we have to face living in a mature, grown-up way and let our life be full of purpose, our actions have meaning and our existence be fruitful. That's why it's so disheartening to see mothers allow everything else under the sun to fill up their minds, prevent them from thinking. That's why it's so wrong for mothers to dissipate themselves on stupid worthless chatter or become addicts of movies, radio and tabloids.

No, we don't have to enter a convent to combine work and prayer and do all we do for the glory of God and the salvation of souls, especially in our case, the souls in our own household. We just work at being a loving mother.

There is one cue in particular, a danger signal which mothers should watch for. Beware the words, "Go 'way, don't bother me!" Of course, children should not be spoiled, pampered, catered to as though mother were a lackey and the child a king, but something is amiss when mothers are always seeking ways to "chase them away" either to a movie or a friend's house, or elsewhere to play. Blessed is the mother who gives in a well-balanced, cheerful and wholesome way her thought and time and life for her children.

Fathers

As to fathers, everything there is to say about fathers can be summed up thus, "The husband should be the head of the house." Simply because this expression is bandied about and joked over today we no longer have any concept of what it means and what it entails. No ruthless tyranny, no bloated, beastly authority substitutes for fatherhood. The divine plan for fatherhood makes it a sacred thing. If we rightly understood the sense in which the husband is the head of the house and the wife the heart we would know why a certain Trappist priest said, "If I had my way, vigil lights would be burned before married couples."

One spiritual writer has described the family as a little church with the father as the bishop.

Coming down to plain, everyday existence, let us face the fact of father's first place. The father rightly should be the provider and mainstay of the family but his vocation consists of far more than that. It is not enough to bring home a pay envelope and consider his obligation fulfilled. He should be more than a provider just as the other should be more than a housekeeper and nursemaid. He must shoulder the responsibilities in managing home and family, should take the initiative in new ventures in the development of the family and its progress and welfare. It is so wrong for a husband to leave all the decisions, all the responsibilities, all the thinking to the wife. If God had not wanted marriage to be a partnership, he could so simply have created one sex.

Yet there are homes where one partner must do the work of two. Usually it is the woman, but she can never really be father and mother both. Many heroic souls carry this burden bravely but usually everyone suffers from it. The children are deprived of well-balanced homes and a real father. The mother weighted down with more than her share often suffers physically and mentally. The man, not fully living his manhood, is debilitated and whatever front he brags remains weak and undeveloped in character.

Some of the blame lies on women themselves, mothers who brought their sons up pampered and spineless, wives who want to run the whole show themselves. Yet there are men who deliberately shirk the duties of the "head of the house." The nation is full of them settling the affairs of the world and big league baseball over their beers, disdaining as beneath them their kingship at home.

But a home must have its head. Authority is necessary to order and life. The mother having a twenty-four hour day job in her own realm needs a wise head and a good heart beside her. The children need a father to fill the place God made for fatherhood in their lives. And Dad must be more than a good sport, he must be a good soul. Our children's first world is—mother, father, home. If we teach them to say "Our Father Who art in heaven," they ought to have a decent meaning for the word "father" and where else will they learn it but from their personal experience with their father on earth. If we teach them to call God "Our Father," then *father* must be a tremendous living force else the word is a mockery, perhaps a blasphemy.

Once an agnostic acquaintance told me he could never "accept" the fourth commandment. He added bitterly, "If you knew what associations the word has for me, you would never ask me to call God 'Father.'" Granted all fathers may not cause such a poisonous reaction in their sons. But how many have been such a negative quantity in their children's lives that whole generations have grown up never quite making any sense out of calling God their "Father."

They do not think of God as the Source of Life when they regard only vaguely and perhaps in a most accidental way their own father's part in bringing them to life. They cannot imagine God providing for them, nurturing them, solicitous for them, protecting them, supremely interested in their affairs, tenderly possessing them, even laying down His life for them, when their earthly father was hardly the type to do these things. Can we expect our children to have faith in a heavenly Father Whom they cannot see when they can't even have faith in the only father they do know?

The head of the house ought to be in his own human way and in his earthly realm the father, as God is the Father in His divine way and supernatural realm. Reams have been written on motherhood but there is still too little said today on the place and importance of fatherhood. Yet just as a mother ought to be the doorway through which a child first sees Mary, mother of us all, so a father should be the portal through which the child first glimpses God, Creator and Father of us all.

Adorers of God

As for "bringing up children" there is only one way to do it: *bring them up to God.*

It often seems the biggest part of raising them is the moral and discipline part—bringing them up to be good or bad, polite or ill-mannered. Now I do not wish to minimize the importance of morality, nor could I. But really morality ought to be an effect of religion and not the sum total of it.

We would not have such a terrific time with "good and evil" if we worked at making our children God-conscious and God-loving.

When I was a child my mother often said of me, "She is always good....She never gives me any trouble." What my mother didn't know was that she had inspired such a love in me for her that I couldn't bear to do anything to offend her. I considered her feelings first, and far above my own. If she bought me a dress I didn't like, I would exclaim over it and admire it. I might be miserable wearing it but would have been more miserable if I had turned away from her gift and spoiled her pleasure in giving it to me. Interrupt play to run errands? Her wishes and needs and desires were more important to me than all the games and playmates in the world. Mind the younger children, help in the house? Naturally. Disobedience? It never occurred to me. The idea of disobeying would have been repulsive. I loved her and would suffer if she were hurt in any way. Serving her was as natural and as easy as breathing.

Cannot parents inspire in their children such a love of God that they will think only of pleasing Him, of serving Him and all this in a joyful, easy way?

Of course, there will always be the pressure on them (and us too) of the effects of original sin, so they are not going to be perfect or even near it. But God supplies the graces we need to counteract those effects. And once they have received Holy Communion they have a daily source of strength. There will be routines of prayer, even simple prayers, morning and night, grace at mealtimes. Later when they are ready for it they join in the family rosary.

The way to lead them is the way of love. God gave us ten commandments, most of which are "thou shalt not..." Yet he summarized them in just two, and these are "thou shalt love the Lord Thy God and love Thy neighbor as Thyself." So we should teach them to love God and they will love His law, His Will. They will not be so often beset with temptation to evil when their hearts are intent on doing good.

And all this is only the beginning. We want them to become "adorers" of God. This is the easy part, believe it or not. We don't wait until they start school and are handed a catechism. It starts with their earliest years. While they are "under our feet" in the kitchen we go about preparing meals, doing the dishes, but talking to them of God, of the purpose of life, of the Redeemer Who opened the gates of Paradise for them. Children in their baptismal innocence have an unsmudged in-

EQUITY

The Williams and the Fullers
    Were out for real estate.
The Williams got eight rooms for two,
    The Fullers two for eight.

telligence and can easily grasp the ideas in the Real Presence, the Holy Eucharist, the Incarnation.

When we tell them stories we need not neglect Goldilocks or Winnie-the-Pooh (and Winnie is good for laughs) but we should lean heavily on stories of the lives of the saints (how they love to hear about Francis of Assisi!) and incidents in the life of Christ. The nativity story is one they love (and play) the year round. They should learn hymns too. Most children enjoy singing. Hymns make good lullabies.

And in how many ways we can remind them of the power

and majesty and goodness of God: in blue skies and white clouds, in rain, in snow, in the variety and quantity of snow-flakes, blades of grass, trees and leaves of trees, in every living thing about them. "See that great bridge that holds trains and cars and people...see how God has made men that they can build such things." When we point out a boat or a house or other works of man it is always, "Wasn't God good to make men so they can do these things and *do* do them?"

A soul can spend a lifetime studying, contemplating, learning of God and still never exhaust itself. Our children can learn early to see the design of God in everything about them. They can so effortlessly become constantly recollected in God. How they will adore Him! And knowing Him and serving Him will be a joy not a drudge. Love makes all things possible. As they become true lovers of God they will not falter at adversities that beset them later. Sacrifice, self-de-nial, mortifications which invariably must be faced in life will not be met with resentment, frustration and neuroses.

Putting God first in their lives will do more toward making them normal, happy human beings than all the psychology books ever written. It will give them a right sense of values for all time and will be the base and foundation on which they stand. In the future too, whatever vocations and careers they pursue their life will have purpose and direction. All this is not intended as a mere piety pep talk. It is too vital to be dismissed as such.

Actually we have an *obligation* to do this much for our children. A glance at all the messy lives around us ought to quicken us at the task, for if ever a people have been diverted from God, we have been.

We will not consider at this time ourselves, the grown-ups. Let us draw a curtain of shame over that category for now. But what of the youngsters?

"Restless, O Lord!"

How can we look upon the tragedy of our future wives and mothers attending theatres and literally screaming in pseudo ecstasy at a radio singer? What do you think of the tender souls who live in make-believe worlds where Hollywood idols sate their dreams and desires? I recall a nine-year-old who came to our house and amidst sighs and limpid gesturings spoke of the god-like man she worshipped on the screen. These faraway mortals held her enraptured, body and soul. It was enough to sicken you heart and make you weep. As these children grow older they carry on in their imaginary world and confuse it with reality; through such a blur they transfer their affections to nearer mortals and new creatures. Boys and girls engage in adolescent but passionate romancing, have crushes on public characters of dubious repute, are obsessed with sports, amusements, cosmetics, clothes, books. I mean obsessed truly in the sense that these "creatures" are given time and consideration and devotion out of all normal proportions. But, it is said, they'll eventually marry and settle down. Indeed? And join our generation of divorce, re-marriage, broken homes, neurotic children?

Well, what can parents do? Restrict movie attendance? Be stricter in supervising their activities? These are methods of handling a disease. The right way is to prevent the disease from taking hold. Hence the purpose in having them God-conscious and God-loving.

For all these vain obsessions are only wild, weed-like growths on souls which should have been basking in the sun of God's light and bringing forth good fruit. And restless and dissatisfied they will be, wasted their lives, if all their growth is away from God for Whom they were created. And all their energies and talents and gifts will end in barrenness or in evil fruits.

Parents have indeed the obligation of telling their children the truth about life. And the truth about life is that we are made for God and will know no rest or happiness until we are centered in Him, till our love is brought to bear on Him.

And woe to us if our children must go through empty searching years, needlessly suffering turmoil and wasted pain only to discover when youth is gone and life is spent the happiness their hungering hearts had craved. Let it not be said of us that because we neglected to tell them from the start our children will someday discover the Divine Lover and cry out with remorse as did Augustine: "Too late have I loved Thee! Too late have I known thee!"

Now is the time to lead them to the Divine Lover. And as we feed and clothe their bodies let us give the best to their souls. Encourage frequent if not daily Communion that their souls be nourished with the Body of Christ and clothed with the raiment of God.

And if your children have those sensitive hearts that are stirred by the splendors of sunsets and moved by beautiful music to know a loneliness overpowering them and an ache within them, you can tell them the truth, that at such moments they are getting cloudy glimpses of the beauty their souls seek and only when they achieve complete union with their Maker will the loneliness be gone and the pain of longing gone with it.

Fill Heaven with Saints

This can mean only one thing, that our work is not done until death, until they are in heaven. So we may even still be at it in the next world if we arrive there before they do (which is the usual thing).

You see, it is not a tidy matter of dismissing our responsibility when they come of age in the world's count of years, when they marry, when they go their separate ways. The parish priest does not cross off his list those aged twenty-one and over, for his is a lifetime work with many souls. Ours is a lifetime work with a few specific ones.

Parents are often confronted with sickening failures in their grown-up children. A son turns out a drunkard, a daughter falls away from the Faith, another perhaps will enter into a bad marriage. What are we to do? Feel sorry for ourselves? Nag and scold them? Tell the neighbors and relatives our child (or children) is breaking our hearts?

Well, we should counsel and admonish them if it will do any good. But what we really must do is pray and sacrifice and do penance and make reparation—and in *secret, unobtrusive ways.* We must suffer for the souls of our children! The price of salvation is suffering. We should pay it, buying their souls with our pain and sorrow and even, when the time comes, our death.

Sounds rough? Hard to take? I'll admit it's a far cry from just washing, ironing and cooking for them.

But think of the Trappists and similar Orders, the cloistered nuns, the priests, the religious brothers and sisters all over the world who are living lives of sacrifice, hard work and reparation for souls, for souls they very often do not know and will never meet this side of heaven. Is it too much to ask of us, that we do as much for the souls we brought into existence, our brothers and sisters in Christ whom we refer to as "our own flesh and blood"?

Or will we, mother and father, be Adam and Eve to our children as our first parents were to all of us? Will they lose Paradise because we would not win it for them?

And how to get them to heaven? It will depend even more on what we are than what we do. You have heard it said that we cannot give to others what we haven't got to give. And every teacher will admit he has always to be a page ahead of his students. So making saints of them means we must become saints ourselves. There's nothing fantastic in that.

But it does mean in forming their characters we'll have to straighten out our own. If they require chastisement, let's not balk at being at least equally severe with ourselves. While we are finding fault with them we can examine our own consciences—and being cheerful with it all! "Joy is the echo of God's life in us."

Do you recall the story of the Curé of Ars who spent as much as eighteen hours a day in the confessional and how people flocked from all over France to him? How did he get that great power of healing souls? Just by sitting there hearing confessions all day? No. It was the remaining hours he spent before the Blessed Sacrament, the penances he inflicted on himself, the work he did on his own soul. He became a channel of God's grace. He emptied himself of self and left room only for God, and so God could work through him.

And so it is with us. Our "eighteen hours daily" are perhaps our actual day's work and activity but behind that must be the work of God. We too must become channels through which God's grace can flow to others, particularly our children. It means we must root out petty whims, faults, selfishness, self-centeredness, all our vices and vanities; clean out our hearts; empty ourselves of every despicable, worthless, nasty trait. It won't be easy. We may in fact be doing it for the rest of our lives and never quite complete the job. But we have to keep at it. We will be wells holding God's refreshing waters for our children. We must not let those waters be muddied or contaminated.

Have you ever seen a child present an awkward, ill-made

product of his own handiwork as a gift to his parents? Poorly finished and smudged with finger marks it is, yet his parents understand the effort and motive behind it and the love it represents. Have you ever seen a child make such a present for his father? And mother first took it and cleaned and beautified it and wrapped it attractively before it was presented to father?

We, too, are but clumsy children with our limited intelligences and skill and we are trying to fashion these souls for God. But when the work is finished Mary will bring it to Him with us—but first she will add her own lovely finishes and we will hardly recognize the magnificent gift it becomes. And our loving Father will at last bring their souls to ultimate perfection. God always rewards good parents.

Rhythm:
The Unhappy
Compromise

Children today are optional. Whether one wants them or not can be a deciding factor in how many one has or doesn't have. This is a fact peculiar to our times. It presents moral problems rarely encountered in other centuries. The element of human prudence in the matter of regeneration has become increasingly important as science has discovered more and more about the biology of humans. The fact that many of our mothers and most, if not all, of our grandmothers let nature take its course, is not so praiseworthy when one considers that they had no conscious alternative. Continence for supernatural motives, which presupposes heroic virtue in both husband and wife, never was and never will be popular. The only controls over the conception of life afforded to the multitudes have been natural and unnatural birth control, and these methods have only been popularly understood in our times.

The Catholic is no less aware of this element of choice

than is the pagan. He knows, however, that artificial contraception is gravely sinful. If this is his only reason for avoiding it, then it is not at all surprising that a substitute technique somewhat less reliable but not in itself sinful would find him a ready disciple. It is in this guise that the technique called Rhythm is being propagated. The zeal of some of its Catholic advocates would do justice to the crusader. The attitude current among many of the younger Catholic couples is that Rhythm is a recommended practice, verging upon a precept. On more than one occasion Catholic friends have told us that it is more Catholic to plan families by the use of Rhythm than to take children as they come!

Since it has become a matter for human prudence, and because much of the education on the subjects is recommendatory rather than cautionary, we have enlisted the capable and qualified services of Father Hugh Calkins, who weds wisdom with experience in *Rhythm—The Unhappy Compromise.*

Rhythm: The Unhappy Compromise

Hugh Calkins, O.S.M.

What about Rhythm? That simple question is rapidly becoming a stormcenter of controversy. It comes up during parish missions, Cana Conferences, bull sessions on careers, even high school retreats. All too often, wrong answers are given, bum theology is handed out. Even more often, right answers are given but very imprudently. These cause confusion among the laity and lead to cynical questioning. Why don't priests get together on this thing voices that cynicism.

This article will discuss Rhythm thoroughly. First, the latest and best theological thought concerning the morality involved shall be presented. This will remove the guesswork of beauty shop theologians and gabfest experts who too easily settle everything with: "Oh, Rhythm's okay. It's Catholic birth control." Secondly, we shall present the true picture of how Rhythm is currently being used around America. It is not a pretty picture, but it's based upon wide missionary experience and thorough research. It may surprise a few too glib advocates of Rhythm—lay, cleric, religious—to see how widely astray Catholic couples have gone on this moral question. Thirdly, we shall discuss how all this fits into a full Christian life, into the synthesis of religion and life any earnest Christian must promote, if we are "to restore all things in Christ."

Moral Considerations

Let's understand what we mean by Rhythm. Incidentally, we are permitted to discuss the method. The only official prohibition issued by the Church deals with the teaching and recommending of the method. Too long have we kept silent, while imprudently zealous advocates spread the method nationwide. The term Rhythm is a convenient name for a systematic method of performing marital relations on certain days of the month. The method is built around the Rhythm of fertility and sterility which occurs in the monthly cycle of a woman's menstrual periods. Briefly, it now seems medically certain that on certain days of the month a woman is quite likely to conceive new life and on other days she is quite unlikely to conceive. The days on which conception are quite likely are called "fertile": those on which conception is quite unlikely are called "sterile." The Rhythm Method consists in following a systematic method of performing marital relations only on "sterile" days and abstaining on "fertile" days. This method is followed in order to space children or to avoid having children. Whether the method is used for a few months, a few years, or all during childbearing years, the motive remains the same. The motive in using this method is to avoid conception and pregnancy. Let's have no talk about "virtuous continence." That's the red herring often dragged in to confuse the issue. The people who use Rhythm are not primarily concerned about continence. They seek to avoid conception. Hence, they restrict sexual intercourse strictly to sterile days, safe periods.

Contrary to widespread misunderstanding, Rhythm is not the same as contraception. It's true that often the aim of the married couple is the same—they use Rhythm to avoid conception—but their method is not the same as the birth-controller. The practice of Rhythm is natural so far as the biological aspect is concerned. The practice of contraception is unnatural, against nature, a perversion just as truly as homosexuality. But just because Rhythm is "natural" doesn't mean it is always morally good and permissible. The practice of Rhythm proceeds from a free and deliberate will—the will not to have children—that is directly opposed to the primary purpose of marital relations as ordained by God. Is such a free will choice contrary to the will of God and sinful?

Without getting too technical, there are two schools of thought on the essential morality of Rhythm as a system. The more common opinion, the majority opinion, holds that this method is not of itself illicit, and becomes lawful only when there is sufficient cause present for sidestepping the primary purpose of marriage. Both opinions are approved by expert theologians: you may follow either one until the Church makes an official pronouncement on the subject. But keep in mind that all theologians hold certain basic facts to be true. There is perfect agreement among theologians that Rhythm can become sinful because of circumstances and dangers involved.

Important Conditions

So we can summarize the latest and best theological thought on the subject. The Church neither approves nor disapproves of the Rhythm Method as a system to be followed. The Church merely tolerates the use of this method.

Tolerates indicates reluctant permission. And the Church only tolerates this method, when three definite factors are present. These three are: *First*, there is sufficiently serious reason for a given couple to use this method, sufficiently serious enough to justify side-stepping the first purpose of marriage; *Second*, both husband and wife are truly willing to follow the method—neither one can force the other to adopt this system; *Third*, the use of this method must not cause mortal sins against chastity nor become a proximate occasion of such sins. The breakdown of any one of those three factors makes the use of Rhythm sinful. So the correct attitude is this: The use of Rhythm is sometimes no sin, sometimes venial sin, sometimes mortal sin. Please stop saying, "Oh, it's okay, the Church approves it."

Now study carefully those three factors. First, a sufficient reason; theologians admit there are at times solid reasons to justify the use of the Rhythm system. These reasons may be permanent or only temporary—poverty, poor health of the mother (real, not pretended), frequent still-births or Caesarean births, medical necessity of spacing births because

MODEL T FOR TWO

We will raise a family,
    A Ford for you, a Ford for me.
Then you'll see how childless
    We will be.

of the unusual fecundity of the wife, in other words, solid and honest reasons for avoiding births for a time, or maybe for all time. But even when such honest reasons are present (and so often today they are not) it still remains true that husband and wife must both be truly willing.

But all too often in actual daily life, one spouse is unwilling and is being high-pressured by the other. All moral theologians would condemn as a grave sin the exclusive use of the sterile period when it is not a truly free agreement on both sides. If not free, a grave injustice is done the other spouse. Such dangers and such mortal sins are frequent in our materialistic age. Confessors would do well to investigate the close relationship between "cheating" by married people and their use of Rhythm. So a good reason by itself is not enough. Circumstances change cases. A confessor's help is advised. More about those three factors later.

Assuming there is free consent and no special dangers of mortal sin, would a couple be justified in using Rhythm for only selfish reasons? Theological opinion is divided: some say such a course would be mortally sinful, others say venially sinful. But all eminent theologians say such a course would be sinful and fraught with grave danger. The more you study the theologians on this question, the more you see how cautious priests and laity should be in advocating Rhythm. You see why the Holy See, only with reluctance, tolerates this method. It certainly has never been declared officially that the Holy See approves of the "safe period" method. Not even the much-quoted paragraph from the "Chaste Wedlock" encyclical of Pius XI can be accurately used as giving such approval. It is far more likely that Pius XI was referring to physically sterile people ("certain defects") or those who have passed the menopause ("reasons of time") and not the use of Rhythm. Yet the new supercolossal campaign for selling Rhythm devices by mail dares to quote the Holy Father in approval of such crassly commercial restriction of birth.

Face the Cold Realities

Now that we've laid the theological groundwork, let's be terribly practical. Catholic couples have gone hog-wild in the abusive employment of Rhythm. Theological distinctions have been pitched completely in the utterly selfish desire to avoid conception at any cost. Too many priests are acting imprudently in the public recommendation (in classrooms and sermons) of the method which the Holy See has cautioned "the confessor may cautiously suggest." There is abundant evidence increasing daily that only spiritually strong couples can be trusted really to observe Rhythm prudently, even when a sufficient reason is present. All too many other couples say they're using Rhythm and they really are following a system of "Don't become pregnant at any cost." So they use Rhythm, when it "works," varied methods of contraception when it doesn't work, and even abortion when they get "caught" (what an expression to describe the start of an immortal existence). Yet all the time such people try kidding confessors with "Oh, no, no birth control, we just use Rhythm."

It's becoming a scandal to their sincere neighbors. John Doe is no theologian. He doesn't make fancy distinctions between unnatural and natural birth control. All he sees is these selfish couples are married and don't have kids—even brag about how they're through having any more. He begins to wonder how they can so easily go to Confession and Communion. I'm beginning to wonder too. Even our adversaries throw a body blow at us by saying: "What's the difference? You forbid contraception so firmly, but your couples slip through by using Rhythm."

Promoting Sterility

The thing is out of hand. A method meant to be a temporary solution of a critical problem has become a way of life, a very selfish, luxury-loving, materialistic way of life. What theologian would ever justify practices like these actual cases I now cite: parish priests giving a copy of a book on Rhythm to each engaged couple with a word of approval; preachers explaining in weekend retreats the advantages of this method for having children as you planned them; teachers in some of our best colleges teaching the method, often to girls who are well set financially; gynecologists lecturing in leading Catholic medical schools and telling classes of young doctors how to teach this method to patients, so that the doctors assume Church approval to recommend the method has now been given them; engaged couples planning their wedding day with rhythm cycle all plotted so no pregnancy results until a year or two passes, so that they can enjoy all the privileges and none of the obligations of marriage.

It is one thing to permit Rhythm reluctantly, as the Church officially does. It's quite another to become promoters of sterility, as too many of our people have. Naturally, the commercializing of Rhythm has hit a new high. Expensive gadgets are now available—"every medical and theological student, nurse and social worker should have one," reads the blurb. So now our people have fool-proof methods of "making love by a calendar," effectively blocking God's creative designs. It's enough to make God vomit out of His mouth the creatures who ignore so completely the divine purposes of marriage. How will we ever convert godless America, how produce modern saints, if we won't give God citizens for His Heavenly Kingdom? And most ironic of all, Catholics so anxious to be in on Catholic Action (which to them means anything from bingo to flag-waving) are often the most determined advocates of Rhythm. They labor so hard to get others to attend lectures, Cana Conferences, book reviews; but to have babies as God wants them to—don't be silly. Have you noticed the heavy emphasis on Rhythm among our wealthy parishes, among our college graduate couples, our social and cultural leaders?

Rhythm Mentality

So there has sprung full-grown from pagan propaganda this vicious Rhythm mentality—a state of mind that won't trust God. Our moderns concede God knows how to balance the universe in the palm of His hand, knows how to harness atomic energy, can dangle stars and planets at His fingertips, but children? Oh, no, God just doesn't know how to arrange things there. We'll take care of that through family planning. But the planning centers about *how not* to have a family. So our do-gooders extol either the practice of total sexual abstinence (oh, so piously), even when the other partner is unwilling and is being unjustly defrauded, or the practice of methodical Rhythm. They don't admit or don't care about the mortal sins such systems produce. They are determined: No Pregnancy Now! There is the state of mind that despairs of God's help.

These bleeding hearts, especially busybodies-in-law, and nosey neighbors, scream protestingly: "Who'll take care of the next baby?" The simple answer is: The same God that takes care of you even when you resist His Will. "But we must give our children security and education." Just because God doesn't give parents and children all today's phony materialistic standards require, doesn't mean He fails them. He didn't give His own mother much in material security. But heaven, not security, is the goal set for the babies God sends. God established marriage primarily to give children life in this world that would bring eternal life.

Too many people are trying to play God. God alone is still the Author of new life. And God doesn't need alarmist doctors, despairing parents, nor even thoughtless priests trying to run His affairs and deciding when new life shall be born. What God wants from us is free will co-operation with His Will. That's the one contribution we alone can make. What God demands from married partners is willingness to have the children He shall decide to send. People go to heaven only by doing God's Will, not by planning things for Him.

Well, then, should every couple have a flock of children? That's up to God. Every couple should have the children God wants them to have. But they are not having them. Forty-four percent of American families have no children. Twenty-two per cent have only one child. And Catholics living in cities now have far fewer children than the families in rural areas (which are about eighty per cent Protestant). Obviously, family planners are planning families out of existence. That certainly is not God's Will. The use of Rhythm by so-called "devout" Catholics is a major factor in that falling birth rate. You say the birth rate is up higher now? Yes, on the first and second babies. But it continues to fall steadily in the number of third, fourth and later babies.

Too Much Prudence

The Rhythm mentality has a tear-jerker argument. It's turned on, full stops, something like this: "But God wants people to use prudence in bringing children into the world. Neither God nor His Church demands people have as many kids as possible. People should use discretion, be decent enough to plan their family. Isn't it far better that a few kids be well fed, clothed, educated than a large family endure poverty." It sounds good, doesn't it? People advancing this line are often quite righteous about it. With pharisaical smugness, they feel sorry for "imprudent pregnancy" of poor parents. But I'm sick of them. They're the kind who probably pitied Mary of Nazareth, carrying a Baby God has sent, but for whom Joseph and Mary couldn't find a home (talk about a housing shortage and tough landlords). They're the kind who pitied my own mother, when she carried me, her twelfth child. Sweet chance I, and many another poor kids like me, would have to be priests, if Rhythm mentality prevailed. And what would the bleeding heart of another day have done about Nancy Hands carrying the Baby who became Abe Lincoln? There would have been no Bernadette of Lourdes, coming from a jail flat, nor Teresa of Lisieux from sickly parents and a mother who lost three babies in a row, and most certainly not a Catherine of Siena, a twenty-third child, if the "prudent planners" had their way. What all these extollers of prudence forget is: God's Will is the end of man. The essence of the world: ours to do His Will. Prudence is a cardinal virtue, highly praiseworthy indeed. But faith, hope, and charity are supernatural virtues far more praiseworthy. *And the greatest of these is charity.* What nobler way to practice charity than to co-operate with God in passing on new life, when God wants it to be born, not when humans think it should? Let only God play God.

Hidden Costs

"Such a manner of using the marriage right, followed without a very serious reason during all, or almost all of the married life, is opposed to the plan of Providence for the propagation of the human race, represents a serious attack on the honor of marriage and particularly on the dignity of the wife, and creates grave dangers for the married people." So spoke the Bishops of Belgium in their Fifth Provincial Council back in 1937. Their words point up the hidden costs of using Rhythm. Take that point on debasing the honor of marriage and lowering the dignity of the wife. Fifty per cent of today's mothers are neurotic, say several leading non-Catholic psychologists. In many cases, Rhythm produces the neurosis. It made the "rejecting mother" type. She "got caught" with a pregnancy she had sedulously fled. The unwanted pregnancy results in the lonely, neurotic, unwanted child. Neurosis like this can increase sterility, so often when the "Rhythmeer" finally wants a baby, she can't have one. It's odd that women can't see the debasing results of a system that uses them systematically to satisfy sexual desires but seldom to produce children.

Advocates of Rhythm are fond of stressing how "natural" the method is. But as Father Lavaud, O.P., has said: "We cannot see an adaptation to nature in something which is, in effect a trick to frustrate nature." Rhythm is quite unnatural as currently employed. It requires the couple to "make love by a calendar," so charts, gadgets, graphs rule romance, not the loving desire of devoted partners. Some medical men assure us a wife's desire for marital union is most vehement precisely during the fertile period. It appears the Jews followed a more natural procedure in abstaining during sterile

**FROM THE FRYING PAN
INTO THE FILE**

**"We'll never be dictated to,"
They told their Toms and Jerrys,
So out they went with noses high
And worked as secretaries.**

periods, as the Book of Leviticus indicates. Even Dr. Ogino, the originator of the method, viewed the method primarily as a means of having children. "Rhythm in reverse," having relations on fertile days just to have children, is natural.

Another hidden cost is infidelity. Women puzzled by male misbehaving at certain time periods might well remember the desires of the flesh respect no calendar. And remember, too, man's sexual life follows a monthly cycle of vehemence and subsidence, as well as a change of life later. Men not living a properly satisfactory sexual life with wives, too much calendar restriction, are easy victims to feminine wiles outside the home. The coolness and jittery bickering caused by Rhythm is incalculable. The fulfillment of marriage as a vocation demands that husband and wife minister to each other's needs through tenderness and understanding often best expressed through love-making and intimate union postponed by the Rhythm calendar. How stupid to live a love-life holding your breath.

Who shall estimate the hidden costs generated in a woman's finely adjusted emotional and psychical life through fear of having another baby. Once such fear is implanted, how difficult to eradicate it. How easily it leads to desperation about avoiding pregnancy at all costs. Be sure that Satan knows how to employ it to create despair about trusting God. Only in eternity shall we know the immortal souls denied a chance to have life because they were snuffed out through abortions caused by such fear.

The New Synthesis

What's the answer to all this bogeyman propaganda about babies? It could be expressed in a word *Vivant* (*let them live*). One group of splendid parents in Milwaukee have taken that word as their slogan and the title of their magazine circulated among young married couples. It's a vivid expression of the forgotten virtue of hope. God's providence still rules the world. True Christians, mindful of their supernatural birth at Baptism, the growth of that life of grace through Mass, Sacraments and prayer know that hope not only springs eternal but it brings eternity as its reward. It devastates right here on earth the creeping paralysis of despair born of these hard times. It cures insecurity by abandoning itself to the constantly supporting arms of God. Married couples, so fearful of what to eat and wear with children arrived or coming, need frequent meditations on that famous sixth chapter of Matthew: "Seek ye first the Kingdom of God and His justice, and all these things shall be added unto you." Seeking His justice means doing His Will, doing it with hope in your heart that God will provide and reward generosity. He never is outdone in generosity, as we all should know from experience. Surprising how God fills your heart and life with pulsating affection of children, once you trust Him enough to have the children. Surprising how little warmth there is in the mink coat, the vacation, the television set, the car that you fought so hard for, while denying your arms the warm embrace of children. Or is all this surprising? God keeps His word.

It would be well to meditate frequently on Paul's vivid reminders about "the great Sacrament" married people give each other on their wedding day. Matrimony joins two hearts and souls and lives by fusing natural and supernatural bonds that day. God and husband and wife become partners that a great vocation might be fulfilled. The virtue of hope receives a mighty increase that day through the grace of Matrimony. At every instant of their married life, the married couple has God's assurance that His grace is sufficient for them. No obstacle is insurmountable to God.

As Father Orville Griese, in his famous book, *The Rhythm in Marriage and Christian Morality*, says:

> Christian couples ought to realize that it is a singular, providential blessing to be able to bring forth new life, thus assuring man and wife of a deeper, most lasting union, offering them means of personal sanctification and of contributing to the strength and growth of both Church and State. The mere fact that the future looks a little uncertain or that the child might be frail or sickly is no reason for substituting faith in the biological computations of the safe period method for trust in God.

THE ONLY CHILD

SEAN O'FEARGHAIL

The young boy stared vacantly at the shadowed wall,
Stared vacantly at the sinewed branches, the curling
Leaves on the shadowed wall.
His lithe form curved limply under the rumpled covers,
Curved limply then straightened, then tossed then rolled,
Then settled under the rumpled covers.

He thought of Johnny and Johnny had Richard and
Richard
Had Mary and Mary had Therese, all in one family.
And he had no one.
He thought of Mother and Mother had Aunt Cel'
and Aunt Cel'
Had Uncle Jim and Uncle Jim had Uncle Bill,
all in one family.
And he had no one.

Except himself—himself was his playmate on rainy days,
Himself drilled soldiers, built forts, visioned legends
In the winter, on rainy days.

The air he breathed was free of germs, sterilized, empty,
Free from all grit, all vapor, the voices of brothers,
Sisters; it was antiseptic, empty.

A desert of loneliness, hedged by dawn and evening,
Preserved by Mother, by Father,
by four rooms, by the new car,
By the gods of the Market Place and their Law—
the Standard of Living.
A gnawing hunger, growing with the fibre and the flesh,
Locked in the soul, poisoning the heart,
shrinking the spirit,
Stirring the mind to incessant fantasy—the Counterfeit of
Friendship.

A wall of silent nonentity, barrier to the human,
Forbidding the warm embrace of innocent youth,
The childish secrets, the impetuous squabbles,
The reality of make-believe—the magic of childhood.

The young boy stared with moist eyes
at the shadowed wall,
Stared with moist eyes at the cross-antlered boughs,
The shifting leaves on the shadowed wall.
"Hail Mary, full of grace,
send me a buddy so we can play,"
Ave Maria, none is more lonely than a lonely child,
Send him a buddy so he can play.

THE CHILD FROM ONE TO HEAVEN

NEIL MACCARTHY

The art of raising Christians requires a deft ability to coordinate and inspire the ordinary techniques of good child care with a single motive: the love and service of God. The secret of this art is simple but not easy: to raise Christian children, you must first be a Christian yourself.

To be Christian is to extend in time the life and work of Our Lord by loving God, living in grace and serving others. This has never been easy. In monasteries it has never been easy. In lay life it is less easy. It is even harder in a decaying and secular society like ours.

To be a Christian parent is harder yet. The family is a group organism. Its growth demands the continual subjugation of the individuals comprising it, lest the interplay of personalities make the home a battlefield. Thus it must often seem that those practices and preoccupations which for the individual prepare the way of perfection, the ascent to Mount Carmel—solitude, recollection, formal prayer—are

submerged when one becomes a parent in the flood of tri-
fling, mundane concerns which characterize the group life.
Sometimes years of resentment must be borne before parents come to see that this perpetual self-sacrifice, far from
smothering their souls, has softened their egotistic bent for
personal spiritual success with those traits of abandon, supple-
ness in circumstances and dependence on the Will of God,
which are the mark of truly Christian souls. Parenthood requires a constant preoccupation with the physical needs of
one's family and therefore a stake in the things of this world.
To organize efficiently the minutiae of daily life and yet keep
alive the love of each member of the family for the others
and of all for God is indeed a difficult task.

There are many ministries. Preachers enflesh the Word
in tones that quicken us to faith. Philosophers enshrine the
Word in crystal thought which error cannot cloud. Saints
materialize the Word in heroic action. Priests substantiate
the Word as none of us can by changing bread to Christ.

But parents can make the Word flesh in a unique and
almost literal sense. From the moment they conceive a child
until his last work of degrading or ennobling the world is
done, the work of their hands and hearts can incarnate the
Word as can no other ministry.

Therefore must parents live in grace, lest their ministry
be blamed.

It is so easy for them to be wrong, to misconstrue the
relation of religion to life. They can drift into thinking of
religion as a decoration, a cultural flourish to be added to
"The American way," or as a substitute for life, a drug to
enmist in rosy vagueness the harsh outlines of a wicked world.

Parents who mistake Christianity for a social grace bring
up cynical and secular children who lead shallow, undisciplined lives cluttered with movies, candy, cereal boxtops and

comic books. The failure of these parents is not always recognized. They are reasonable people, a credit to the town,
good friends and neighbors. It is not noticed that they are
not Christians.

Parents who seek "comfort" in religion are more readily
detected as maladjusted. Christianity afflicts these people like
a disease. They are full of tracts and medals and esoteric de-
votions to unknown saints. They entertain the clergy often
and at such times butter their conversation with private un-
derstandings with the Blessed Mother and churchly chitchat
about Father Jamey getting Good Shepherd parish after all.

Such people seldom concern themselves with the merely
natural aids to parenthood, like the PTA or parents' magazines or the Montessori system. Teaching Tommy to use
simple tools or working out a schedule of chores and allowances for him is less important to them that seeing that
Tommy wears a scapular.

Such parents lack a sense of proportion. They are somewhat silly. But they are less reprehensible than the middle-
class type. They do realize that there is a dog beneath the
skin and that the natural order is not to be complacently
accepted as it is.

How do parents who love God and live in grace and
have got straight the connection between religion and life
approach the task of raising Christians?

They begin with a study of sound child care. They know
that the liturgical life is neither a substitute for the world
nor an endorsement of it: it is a *critique*. They use the love of
God as a touchstone, a divining rod by which to select and
transform those things in the natural order which can honor
Him. Therefore they use the ordinary means of learning how
to bring up children. They have no facetious attitude toward

government pamphlets like *The Child From One to Six* or nursery clinics or books on child welfare. They use these aids with discretion, but their approach is careful rather than critical. They have much to learn.

Wise parents begin early to inculcate self-reliance. They allow the walking child to fall down without comforting him. They let him cry a little if he cannot assemble his blocks to his own satisfaction. Occasionally they encourage him with a word or a smile. But as a matter of course, the child is expected to work things out for himself. In doing so, he is strengthened spiritually. Can a Christian be chicken-hearted? Is virtue a valentine of pink bows and baby talk?

Self-reliance can be overlearned. The child trying to walk or shovel sand wants to try it all the time, through naps and meals and other needs. It is here, before the child is one, that wise parents teach a reasonable respect for authority, for Mother's quiet work, for Father's silent look. They do not call out at the child or give in to his whims. They show their dignity by self-control and sensible consistency. The infant learns that No means No. There is no contest of wills, no testing of the strength of No. Mother said "No" or "Bed" or "Give it to me." That is all. It is right, inevitable. When the child is twenty and Mother says, "I want to talk to you, Tom," Tom will come. Mother is probably right. In any event, she is Mother. If Tom gets it into his head to chase women or drink liquor or do any of the things that young men think makes them a real guy, Father can call Tom aside and talk sense to him. But only because the event was prepared for in the playpen and the sandbox.

Thus good Christian parents develop the child from one age to the next. As he grows older, physical problems diminish, moral and spiritual ones increase. Less time is needed for physical projects like bathroom training or throwing a ball or sewing a sock. More time is given to discussion of the ethical situations arising in school, of the nature of the earth and the universe, of basic religious concepts, prayer, faith, grace. But there is no separation of physical and spiritual. When Father shows Tommy how to hold a bat, he may slip in a word about the place of play in the imitation of Christ. Tommy will not pay attention, of course, if he is any kind of a boy. He is too interested in learning the game, in hitting home runs. But there will be hundreds of similar opportunities for Father to make his point. An occasion will present itself to tell the story of the child saint who was playing ball. He was asked what he would do if he had five minutes to live. He replied that he would go right on playing ball. Tommy will unconsciously dovetail this with the other things Father has said. When Tommy is older he will understand the relation of sports to sanctity without knowing how he knows.

Mother is teaching the girls to bake. Little Joan is in tears—her cookies turned out badly. Did you read the recipe carefully, dear? Yes, Mommy—but it seemed like such an awful lot of sugar, I just thought... Mother makes a few, casual remarks about the value of following rules, of paying attention to details. The mailman arrives with a package. It is a beautiful blanket for the new baby. The girls interrupt their cooking to admire the gift. Mother smiles as she reads a motto on the label: "Quality is never an accident." "What is quality, Mommy?" Mother explains. She relates the principle to Joan's cookies. Joan is beginning to learn a lot more than just making cookies....

But this moralizing in situations will seem false and will not be accepted by the children unless, from their birth, they are brought up in a home that radiates affection, idealism and a common life of grace. The infant in his highchair cannot talk yet, but he watches his parents pray before meals.

He wonders what they are doing. Later he imitates the position of the hands. It doesn't matter that he doesn't know what he is doing. It matters only that prayers are as much a staple of existence as diapers or oatmeal.

The Germans have an expression for this principle. They say, "He does not know the words, but he understands the music." That is, the child grasps in an intuitive way many attitudes and meanings. Wise parents utilize this principle in teaching everything. They listen to music and read poems and look at sunsets and pray at Mass, and the child understands only the music. Later, he will learn the words more rationally. But if there has been no music first, the child rightly suspects that what he is being taught is affectatious, not lived out, said for his benefit. Consequently he learns unwillingly and superficially. He does not learn by the blood but by the tongue. And he forgets as soon as he can get away with it—which is often tomorrow. If a child is taught grace before meals with self-conscious airs of piety and coy talk about being a little soldier of Christ, he senses the insincerity of his parents and is led to believe that the whole rigmarole is a gag to fool little kids into being good.

Sincere Christian parents do not produce this reaction. Their children cannot remember a time when Mother and Father were not going to daily Mass or reading spiritual books to each other or discussing current events in the light of Our Lord's teaching. As children grow older and study religion formally, they see they are merely receiving explicit instruction in the facts and attitudes they have always lived by.

Even after catechetical age, the greater part of the children's spiritual instruction goes on at home. Public affairs, heard on the radio and discussed at school, are rehashed at home. What is communism? Why are they after Cardinal Mindszenty? Why do they want to stamp out religion? A

Maryknoll magazine arrives. It features a full-page photo of a ragged Chinese peasant sitting on the ground, crying like a baby in despair and grief. His bony horse stands beside him. There is nothing to eat. Nothing at all. The picture is tacked up on the family bulletin board in the kitchen. The children ask about it. It is explained to them. Why we should pray for the poor and hungry. Why we should eat our own good food with thankfulness. A copy of *Life* magazine lies on the living-room table. Mother fetches it, turns to the section: "*Life* Goes to a Party." She shows the children the pictures of the well-dressed guests, stuffing themselves with delicacies, laughing too much and doing foolish things. She compares them with the Chinese peasant. Is this right? Is it Christian?

Needless to say, wise parents do not sicken their young with an overdose of piety. They take the attitude that God made the world and it is fundamentally good. They inculcate a "relaxed" piety which presumes a Christian viewpoint without tiresomely insisting on it all day long. It is not necessary to evoke the saints hourly, to collect holy pictures, to deck oneself out in the paraphernalia of piety. To follow Christ is to love God and to do everything for His sake—that is enough. God is everywhere: parents need not feel that He can only exist in virtue of their personally planting Him about.

Christian parents, therefore, explain natural and mechanical phenomena reasonably. They discuss the anatomy of rainbows, how radios work, the hydrologic cycle and how babies are born, in a matter-of-fact way , using such aids in the way of blackboards and encyclopedias as they can afford. They are careful, however, to avoid the scientific spirit. The explanation of ant-hills and bee-hives is complete only when it directs the attention of the child to the wisdom and humor and engineering skill of God. Yet the eternal aspect of material things is shown with such a fine sense of proportion that the children are able to talk freely of the things that interest them—frogs and hockey and what Natalie Hubbard did in school—without fearing that the conversation will inevitably veer around to the ten commandments.

As the child enters puberty, all that has gone into his formation is put to a crucial test. The contrast between the ethical pattern by which he has been brought up and the cynical values of the "outside" world becomes more and more obvious. He goes to school, visits the homes of his companions, sees advertisements and billboards and hears the radio, and everything he does and sees and hears shows him plainly that while the rest of the world is "having fun," he is restricted in a thousand ways by the dictates of religion. He has been led to believe that kindness and gentility and love of one's neighbor are natural and expected virtues, and he has behaved accordingly. Now he is called a "sucker." And as he looks at his friends with their pockets full of coins, their movies and soda pop and comic books, he wonders if he is one. His friends don't do chores or go to daily Mass. They can see *Neptune's Daughter*. He is not allowed. Why not? Is he being taken in? Is Catholicism real? Or are the values of the world around him "real"?

Many children are lost forever to their parents at this age. The instinct of the child is to pull away from his elders, to become emotionally independent. It is psychologically necessary for him to do so. If the attitude of his parents is sympathetic and honest, he is enabled to detach himself from them emotionally without rejecting their spiritual pattern. If his training till now has been Christian, his struggle for personal identity will not unduly alarm his parents. They will not try to fetter him with idiotic demands for affection and blind obedience. They are confident they can hold him

with the silken threads of love and respect for their example—
threads which may have an elasticity, which give but never
snap, struggle though he may. Let him thrash his wings a
bit.

Thus wise parents handle this fight for identity, this
youthful war on the outcome of which depends the success
of all their efforts, with tactful understanding. They adjust
themselves to a granting of concessions, a paying out of slack
in the silver cord. But this is never done on a bargaining
basis: you do this and I'll let you do that. The loosening of
the ties that bind presumes the idea of equity—adult behavior meriting adult privilege. And in keeping with this, the
conflict between the child's two worlds, his home and his
outside experience, is honestly faced.

There *is* a difference between life in a Christian family
and the pleasure-seeking existence which is the "American
way." Our neighbors do things which we may not do. There
are things our secular friends see and say and think which
we may not, and still be Christians. This does not mean that
our friends are not worthy people, better perhaps by their
lights than we by ours. But they live differently than we do,
and the difference is important.

Christian parents gain nothing by glossing the facts, by
narrowing the chasm between the following of Christ and
the following of self, as though secularism could be sancti-
fied and Christianity "humanized" and the two somehow be
made to appear the same. They are not. And the time has
come for a frank appeal to the child to embrace the life of
grace and reject the life of self-seeking, knowing the implications of both.

Wise parents give this appeal a positive statement by
stimulating a sense of vocation. They teach their children
the use of the Missal and a real participation in the liturgy of

the Church. They develop an understanding of the Mystical Body, a sense of living the life of Christ by extension in time. The saints are introduced as models of behavior. Their achievements are studied in preparation for feast-days and name-days, first in the little introductions in the Missal, later and more completely in books given as gifts. The children are led to see that saints are people, that a saint is not a special kind of person, but that every person can be a special kind of saint. Here is a saint who was a farmer, this one a mother, that one Chancellor of the Exchequer, here a philosopher, there the founder of an Order. What are you going to be, dear?—I want to be a nurse, a wife, a doctor, a sheep rancher. Do you? Why? Will it help you to serve God and people? You don't know, you just think it would be fun? Think it over, dear, think it over....

Thus, with piety and patience, good parents raise Christians from one to heaven—that the Word may be made Flesh. A hard apostolate, but can they wish less?

Can they wish to raise Quizz Kids, brilliant with the fantastic values of television, atomic physics, jazz and beanies-with-propellers-on-top? Or culture-worshippers, prattling smartly of Picasso, Rouault, Hemingway and Waugh?

Eric Gill asked it rightly: "Do you think good taste can save us? Only one thing can save us. We must desire to be saints."

The achievement of holiness is the work of grace, of Him Who made us and knows what He will have of us. We need not see the fruition of grace in ourselves or in our children. Enough that we try.

But to wish anything less for us or for them is to cheat them of their birthright, deny our vocation, and degrade the sacrament of marriage to the status of an obscene playing with dolls.

Parents and Vocational Guidance

Marion Mitchell Stancioff

Most of us know well enough that a vocation is a calling, but are unaware that a *classic* is one who is called. To be a classic is to belong to a selected number, a class worthy to be summoned by name from among the unnumbered multitude. Being called was anciently regarded with a kind of awe. Recently it has been more fashionable to profess, and a calling is now seldom heard of save in strictly ecclesiastical connection. Vocation or profession, to be called or to speak up, to choose or to be chosen. Between these—as between all words—there is a significant difference.

In the romantic period—but very lately ended—man desired to stand alone; it seemed more in keeping with the captaincy of his soul to profess than to listen for a call. But now the wind has veered again, and man though he is not docile is neither any longer proud; he has become a wavering, uncertain thing plunged to the scalp in anxiety and fractioned by inward disunion. And so, for novel reasons, most of us would really wish to be called by name in the night like Samuel and told what we should do.

However it does not often happen. Usually we try a dozen different things before we find satisfying work in life. Still more often, after hesitating and shifting and worrying for years we end up by doing something we feel is little good to others and even less to us. With the best will in the world we are pulled hither and thither by our tastes and interests, our appetites and curiosities, our ignorance of ourselves and of others, of the nature of work. At last in middle age we drag our disillusioned selves from memories of the vocational pillars of fire embraced in our youth and hitch ourselves to the dullest of posts. Since we know that to keep alive is a duty—as well as a pleasure—we justify the job which irks us by invoking the need to eat. Common sense, like Hegel, always tries to justify necessity. And Christian acceptance, like a good gardener, always tries to make something grow even in rocky soil.

Burying Our Talents

But in spite of common sense and resignation there nevertheless remains at the bottom of our hearts a sorrowful sense of waste. This may be because we overestimate our unused abilities, in which case our sense of waste is spurious. Or it may be that our talents are of a high order and in that case we are failing to obey God's explicit order to make them fructify. We feel cheated because we are cheating. We must hope we are not silly enough to mistake a ten dollar bill for a thousand, yet, were it only a one dollar bill we received, even the smallest gift of God carries with it the obligation to bear increase. The steward in the parable who used his master's money well and the one who buried it in the ground had no

instructions as to what they were to do. They were expected
to work that out for themselves. And when the first was rewarded and the other was reproved they were told: "You
knew you served a hard master." In this business there is no
booklet of instructions and those who are specifically led,
like Samuel and Joan of Arc, are very few.

We know we serve a hard master (although those who
serve without any reserve find their task grow strangely light).
So we must look quickly and see whether we have buried the
talents we were given and if so, whether at this late hour we
can still dig them up and make them pay the dividends this
hard Boss of ours is going to ask for on the day that's drawing near.

That however is matter for another inquiry. Now it is
enough if we try to discover what parents can do to make
children and adolescents aware of their endowments, whether
the family can foster the development and the right use of
this natural capital, and further how much the chance of
success and failure in practical life should influence the choice
of work. These are questions parents ask themselves hundreds of times during the years of their children's growth,
and the answers, which vary with each child, are difficult to
find.

Children Must Learn to Dream

It is often hard to tell what a child does well by nature.
Whether he ought to be a doctor or a deepsea diver. And
even if we do discover it, it may be hard, for lack of time or
money, to help him develop his talent. But one thing parents
can certainly affect is the level of their children's aim. It is in
the dreams of childhood that the achievement of the adult is
born. If we do not, by admiration of fine deeds, learn to
dream high as children we shall not act nobly when we are

grown. If we do not dream of being men, we shall never be men, but merely vegetables or machines. If we do not open the door of the inner world when we are young, and open it habitually, we shall not find it later, and may even deny that it exists. It is the imagination which allows us to conceive worlds beyond the cereal and milk reality of every morning. Unless we are taught to dream—which is to make up our own stories—we shall not know how to live our own lives, but will take refuge in stories ready made by others. We must learn to look for true worlds within ourselves or we shall be drawn into the false worlds invented by the ideas-trade.

Children must learn to dream, but not to day-dream. A sensitive and watchful parent can arouse a child to the sharp distinction between dreaming and kidding oneself. By dreaming one learns to hitch one's wagon to a star; but when one wakes one must make sure one has a wagon and that it's not tied to a tinsel star. That basic honesty which never lets us for one second fool ourselves has to be learned in infancy. A child may and should dream of greatness, whether it be as a saint or a saxophone player; but he must be quite familiar with the fact that for the moment he is neither, and that to dream is weakness unless each day by some small practice— whether of generosity or scales—he tries to integrate dream with reality.

The Principle of Doing One's Best

Some earnest parents think the principle of raising their children's aspirations to the stars applies in spiritual matters only. As every Christian should, they encourage holiness and they hopefully seek to discern signs of a religious calling. (Here we should warn parents against the transference of spiritual ambitions to their offspring. The terrible pressure of a mother's love has foisted many a false vocation on an unfortunate child and on a yet more unfortunate Church.) But if there is no direct call to a religious life, then often these same earnest parents will push their children into the most stupefying jobs. They do not realize that the principle of doing one's best applies in every walk of life, since the world was made by God and all of life should walk in His way. There is a primary vocation to sanctity, which is at the same time a vocation to humanity since the first is the fulfillment of the second. All the world is God's and all the work that is done in it can be done to His taste, that is, perfectly. There is no reason why the man who orders his meditation well or his morals well should not also order his music or his muscles with the same attention.

Ordering implies putting first things first. The would-be saint who sacrifices his sick parent to his passion for the poor is not becoming saintly and the aspiring saxophonist who abandons wife and children for his music will not be fully human. All this parents have the task of making clear to their children, more often by implication than explanation, and with that patient gentleness which alone induces understanding.

Now the child has been led as God intended to dream of doing great things with his life. He has been led further to see that dreams go bad unless they are realized with suitable action and that that always means sacrifice. And he has learned that a dream to which we sacrifice what is not ours to give is a gloomy idol; a dream which turns to nightmare. On this basis of imagination, truth and moral order the child can safely build.

How are these three principles to be applied in a particular family in guiding a specific child to his own lifework? Before examining that question we must pause to answer those people who are still asking whether it is wise in any way to direct a child toward a particular vocation.

Should Parents Give Advice?

Some parents, hyper-sensitive to every chill wind that blows from the playground or the lecture room, hesitate even to advise their children in any way lest they "get their backs up" or "push them down the wrong alley." Often, though pride will not let them show it, children are vastly relieved to get adult advice. Moreover, even if the advice does get their backs up, that may in itself help them to find out what they do *not* want to do. Confronted with the multitudinous variety of the universe it is only human to shrink from choosing. To take only one thing from this board groaning with divers goods is agony to most of us. The horror of free choice, often noted even amongst the most "progressively" educated, needs no other explanation; whereas a little repression, by a process of elimination helps the hesitant child to define his own desires and reach a personal choice. We have been told so often of the terrible dangers of repression; we have not been warned enough that lack of repression leaves the will floating without a chance to put down strong roots. It is essential when planting a seedling to "firm it down" so it will have something to brace itself against; if this is neglected the plant droops and is done for.

Moreover, there are talents which no repression seems able to crush nor is any needed to bring them out. If a child insists on studying mean temperatures or has to be hauled away from the piano, then obviously he should be encouraged to be a weather man or a musician. As clear a call as this saves everyone a lot of trouble. The infant Mozart was called to music as distinctly as Samuel to the priesthood. But most children hear no voice, or at most an inner mumbling which might mean anything and often seems to mean nothing at all. It is those children who most need parents' guidance.

Many, perhaps most, adults do not know what they want to be, and have little desire to be anything at all. Yet as children they wanted to be everything from cowboy to cardinal. Wise parents take advantage of these various stages to direct their children's interest and increase their knowledge. Some youngsters have so much vitality they want to be everything at once. Though confusing to themselves and to their parents, this is a great deal better than lack of interest. Even in the convent St. Theresa of Lisieux still felt she had it in her to be a hundred different things; knew that only by being altogether God's could she be all things to all men. The child with much vitality must be helped to channel his activities effectively and to finish what he begins; while parents will lose no opportunity of stimulating and broadening the interests of their less vital children.

The Problem of Choice

Of course it is only in a society both free and complex—that is to say civilized—that the problem of choice arises. In most societies it does not exist at all or only for certain classes. In an economically simple society a man's career is predetermined by tribal necessity. He is a fisherman or farmer, a hunter or shepherd according to the traditional use of natural resources. And even a highly complex society can, by abolishing freedom and sending a man to the gold fields or the salt mines or picking him to be a stage star or station master, entirely eliminate the problem of choice. No human society is ideally free but the fact that we have a problem of choice to discuss reminds us of that freedom which it is always possible to lose.

There is however, even in a comparatively free society, a considerable economic pressure which limits many in their choice of work. There is a limit to the amount of certain types of work that a society can absorb and parents do well to find out whether the profession which their child is planning to enter is seriously overcrowded and whether it can survive an economic depression. It is also prudent in the case of a career which requires expensive preparation to make sure the child really likes it well enough to stick to it and make the sacrifice worthwhile. Parents have in this matter a difficult double obligation. They must help their children choose a means of earning their bodily living which is at the same time a help and not a hindrance to that development of heart and mind which they need to earn a life.

Success

The chance of success is bound to play a part in the choice of a life's work. Every sane person wants success. There is no question about that. The only question is what kind of success individuals want. Some want to succeed in the service of God and man, some want to be famous for successfully serving, others just want to see their names in the papers. Some people want to win a popularity prize, others want the praise of the "little reviews," and some want to make sure of going to heaven. Here again parents are often able to point out which things are worth succeeding in, while the child is small and before the world has warped the sense of values with which most children come into it. This parents can only effect by example.

Most of us are born with some premonition of that high destiny to which we are all summoned, and have, I suppose experienced at least a few "bright shoots of everlastingness." But now, when most people are spiritual savages, these flashes of mysterious power are often mistaken by the gifted child quite unlettered in spiritual things for the stirrings of human greatness, and to this last but few of us are called. This misunderstanding of his true nature and the consequent deflection of his ambition from a high destiny open to all to a lower destiny open to very few is one of the great miseries of modern man. The urge to greatness as well as the passion for success is given people to help them take the kingdom of heaven by storm. Christian parents who can help clarify his experience are the child's best allies in this campaign which lasts as long as life.

But there have always been a large number of people without taste or color who cannot hope to attain worldly success and must doggedly concentrate on just living, both here and hereafter. Now, besides these there is, thanks to the times, a quickly multiplying race who care neither to please God nor to please themselves. They have turned the Golden Rule upside down. We used to know so well what *we* like that we know exactly what to do unto others—even though we did not often do it. But these other-directed people have no idea of what they like until they have taken a poll of what others like. So they do unto themselves as they think others would do unto them. They do not dare to live at all but merely reflect the show of other lives. They have no ideas until they have ascertained the opinion of everybody else. Such a man is a fleeting picture in a thousand moving mirrors, a mere image in other people's eyeballs. How can these shadows win through to the resurrection? For where there has never been life there can be no life to come.

Dull Jobs and Dull People

It is not these automata spawned by industry and bred by advertising which concern us here, though their existence is a menace to their Christian neighbors. But there are always vast numbers of youngsters without a striking gift or marked tendency of any kind. These young people have to find themselves a preference by a process of trial and error and then cling tenaciously to that, even if it does not satisfy them fully. There are so many dull things to be done in the world, even seen through the eyes of grace. That is one of the things many unrealistic Catholics—as well as all romantic liberals—forget. They tend to assume that every child is a budding artist; that every man, were he not denied self-expression by a harsh system, would fill his days with beauty-bearing labor. But people do not all want to be artists or craftsmen, nor even heal the sick nor delve into the secrets of the universe. Nor do all other activities go against the human grain. This warped wood which the Fall has left us is often better pleased to be around unused than suffer the process of being pressed and spliced and planed to a fine levelness.

Nor is it true that every object made before the industrial revolution was a thing of beauty which gave equal joy to maker and user. Indeed the locksmith in the middle ages often made keys that were beautiful to see, but the beauty was a by-product because the purchaser, having more highly developed personal taste than the modern consumer, liked to show off beautiful possessions—or merely ingenious ones—just as people now like to show off their high fidelity players or their cars. But the locksmith who made beautiful keys chiefly wanted them to work, and if they didn't he lost his job and got one digging ditches. Man loves to tinker as much as to create. He is *homer faber*, and likes to tinker effectively. And he falls in love with his works even when, like machinery, they obviously enslave him more often than they aid him. And even in the middle ages there were quite as many people making chains and pikes and cooking pots as statues for cathedrals. There are always many dull jobs to be done, and there are always people who don't mind doing them. But it is a crime to make work duller than it need be and a sin against the spirit to thereby make people duller. God manages not to find any of His children dull, that is the Father's privilege. But even He has threatened to spew forth those who are neither hot nor cold.

Let fleshly parents therefore take notice and whether their children make or do or merely stand and wait, let parents help them to be more entirely alive in their work and at their play, now and always.

TEACHING CHILDREN TO PRAY

MARY REED NEWLAND

A joke currently booted about over the airways has to do with a small child saying her prayers and teaching, in the *Our Father*, the place where she lisps innocently, "And lead us not into Penn Station." In fact, the attitude towards children's prayers seems to be one of gentle amusement, with now and then a little tear-wiping on the side. A sentimental subject and a popular one, with people who have their children pray. Strangely enough, a lot of people who never bother saying prayers themselves seem to feel that praying has a place in the young child's curriculum, that, for reasons very vague, it ought to be part of their early and most innocent years along with fairies and Santa Claus and Nature Study and the rest.

Yet if there is a time for hard-headed approach to the problem of man's relation to God through prayer, the most perfect time is when the man is still a child. We lather the subject with sentiment and fail to see it in the light of cold logic. We quote glibly, "Unless you become as little children," and fail to see that in their very childhood, children are the most perfectly disposed to accept and understand God and that our job is not to marvel at the simplicity of their faith, the purity of their intentions, but to give them the means to remain as little children by training them in intelligent prayer.

Any prayer, if reverent and with good intention, is acceptable, but how much time is lost and how many precious opportunities passed by for lack of training in prayer. In an age when so much thought is given to proper feeding, all with an eye to insuring the future adult against a variety of physical and social maladjustments, it is tragic that just a small fraction of that energy is applied to insuring against spiritual maladjustment. Why should it be that the majority of men pass from the age of childhood intimacy with God into a long period where the relationship is barely a nodding acquaintance, they find themselves jerked rudely to their knees in the fact of some personal catastrophe and forced to seek Him out all over again in their maturity? And the second seeking out is burdened with guilt of conscience, timidity in the face of long neglect and an almost complete inability to strip the mind of a lifetime recollection of impediments and return to that state of childlikeness where there exists only God and the man, Father and the child.

At the moment of Baptism the climate is perfect for the beginning of a relationship which could be perfect. The Holy Trinity takes residence in the pure tabernacle of the child's soul and he is at once launched upon his spiritual life. A woman once asked the nurse in the delivery room of a Catholic hospital, as she watched her new-born son trundled out to the nursery, "Please say an *Ave* right now that he will never commit a mortal sin." And the nurse, startled, replied, "Say, that's an idea!" Saint Paul says we are called to be saints. The calling becomes a vocation as soon as the child is born. But the problem is not fundamentally the parents'. The business of being a saint, or trying to be one, is always an affair between the single soul and God. The terrible responsibility of the parents lies in their duty to make known the calling to the child, to start him as soon as possible on his journey to God through a lifetime, then through death into eternity. And the first and final steps are through intimacy with God in prayer.

The Sacraments are all-important, of course, but the Sacraments are God coming to us and the reception of them does not necessarily guarantee that we will be saints. For two people to get anywhere with a project both must cooperate, and when one produces the means only to have the other refuse to use them, the project is doomed to end, at best, in mediocrity—even when the first party is God. All we can do for God can be gathered under one label: Prayer. It covers not only the act of praying but all our work, all joy, all sorrow, in fact all our activities, provided they are good ones, if we wish to offer them. The joke of it all is that the end of our giving is in order that He may give to us. So if we are going to run this race as though there were only a single prize, an early start is certainly an advantage. And if we are raising children to win the same prize, of all the provisions we must make for them certainly an understanding in the use of prayer is at the top of the list. It would be sensible, then to establish a pattern of prayer for our children which would serve them without deviation, regardless of the particular circumstances they will meet, during a lifetime.

Too many people underestimate the ability of children

to grasp spiritual truths, yet they will quote innumerable profound remarks their children make and sit back in a puddle of tenderness to contemplate them. It shouldn't be surprising that children make profound spiritual observations: Their souls are pure, filled with the Holy Trinity and the flow of divine grace into them is unimpeded. Granted their mental faculties are not fully trained at the age of four or five, but the relation to God does not depend on the number of hours per week spent in advanced nursery school, or the I.Q. rating, of the quantity of educational toys provided. And just because a poetic adult can contemplate God in the mystery of a blade of grass or the flight of a bird does not mean that the child's awareness of God in these same things is any less intelligent. With the child it is not an intellectual triumph that he sees the proof of God's omnipotence in all the things around him; it is a simple, straightforward fact, which is the fruit of the divine gift of faith in a soul filled with grace. Therefore, if we are wise, we will seize this once-in-a-lifetime opportunity and with the help of God's grace, try to equip our children with an approach to Him which will save them years of half-hearted, aimless effort.

We see, in the light of the various facets of our relationship with God, that we must address Him in a variety of roles: as the child of an all-loving Father, as sinner to Redeemer, as petitioner to the Giver of all things and as grateful recipient of blessings in abundance. Christ pointed this out in the *Our Father* and the same variety of approaches to God are evident in the Mass. Children, at quite an early age, are able to memorize the *Our Father* and the *Hail Mary* but the chances of teaching the meaning of these prayers to any but those with unusual intelligence are remote. However, it is possible to use the general pattern of these prayers and give them a means of conversing with God which will include all the important points and still make sense.

The start is a salutation, of course, whatever form of addressing God is most natural. Then because getting one's sins off one's chest at the very first seems to leave the air purer and the soul freer to enjoy this conversation with God, examen comes next. It is important that the child be left to drag out his little aberrations of his own free will, and don't think they won't remember or they won't admit them. If the parents will make it clear in the beginning that the business of sinning is an affair between the child and God, and not an offense against the parent, it gives them the assurance that revelations in an examen are not going to be interrupted by remonstrances from mother or father. More often than not, a lot of minor mysteries will be cleared up at the nightly examen (for instance, which of our children was pulling the buds off the chrysanthemums—they were locked in mutual and honorable silence when questioned in a group). Then

"COME HERE JUNIOR, AND WE'LL READ ABOUT THE SAINTS!"

comes contrition, "I am sorry, Blessed Jesus, and please help me not to do it again."

And right here pre-schoolers can learn that goodness is something which comes with God's grace and without his help they are apt to do it again and again and again. Some days, of course, are very good days, and the immediate reaction at night prayers is to announce loudly, "I was very good today, God." On the days like this, they can say, "If I did anything today to offend you, I am sorry, I tried very hard to be good." And they are learning to guard against presumption.

Next, petitions: All the "God bless Daddy and help him with his work; God bless Mommy..." and etc., fit in here. And after the most intimate associates are included, some under the heading of "all my family and friends: for the sake of brevity, they learn very easily to include "all the souls in Purgatory, everyone who has been so good to us, everyone in the world and please help the Russian people find God." This latter petition is apt to prompt some interesting discussion and some fabulous conclusions. Jamie announced one night, "I know why the Russian people can't find God. Because He's in our house."

Then comes one of the most important petitions of all. "Please help us all to be saints." To be a saint looks like a fairly easy job to a child, and they have a natural desire to be saints. Only the adult appreciates how hard it is and, looking back, wishes with all his heart he had thought of asking for the necessary graces everyday of his life. We can train our children to—why don't we?

After this comes the break between the affairs of the world and this affair of the heart. "I love you, Blessed Jesus, and I love your Blessed Mother. And I thank You for.....each night a different blessing. The assortment of blessings and pleasures is legion and will include tractors and trucks and ducks and dessert and even, in the case of one of ours, "Thank you for not letting any motorcycles come in our driveway."

Prayers are over and all that is left is tucking in. But with tucking in comes the opportunity to plant a seed that will bear fruit very early in the formation of the habit of meditation, even though the child knows it, not as meditation, but simply as a kind of game called "thinking about." The choice of subjects for thinking about is limitless, but just for the sake of example: "Now before you fall asleep, you think about baby Jesus and how He was just the same size as our Peter, just as sweet and funny, and how beautiful His Mother was. And you think of what it was like there in the barn where He was born, with only the Blessed Mother and Saint Joseph and the cow and the donkey to love Him." It is particularly helpful to remind children that Jesus was just the same size as Jamie at four, the same size as Monica at five, and so on; that He ate three meals a day, and helped His Mother with the dishes, and probably had a cat to feed, and a garden to weed. There are lots of games for children to play which are in reality exercises in meditation. "Looking at the things that God made," is one which helps tremendously to increase their awareness of the vastness of His creation, yet makes the universe a rather snug place because on all sides they find it is filled with things He put there.

Children have such simple faith in the efficacy of prayer that it is easy for them to form the habit of praying on all sorts of occasions...occasions of minor crises during the day when affairs have progressed so far out of reach it becomes quite obvious it is time to turn them over to God. They will voice their prayer aloud, matter of factly, and with the simplicity of the faith that is as a grain of mustard, they wait for the mountain to be moved. One spring day our boys discovered the top to the oil tank was unfastened and dropped two or three dozen rocks in the pipe leading to the tank. I froze, then collected myself enough to attack the delicate job of fishing out the rocks with an old fly swatter handle. They squatted around, very tense, and silent except for an occasional, "Please, Saint Philomena, help Mommy get the rocks out of the pipe." Of course she did. Yet our children are not particularly "pious" types. Nor do we stand around and prompt them. It is very easy to plant the habit, and their world is so much more secure, because of this faith that God is ready and willing to help them on every hand, that calling on Him is second nature to them. I might say, also, that there have been times when some of our cynical and world-wise friends have been more stunned and edified by just calling upon Heaven by the children, in the middle of an ordinary conversation, than they would be if pinned down for an hour's bombardment with learned texts by a zealous adult.

Add to these two other forms of prayer, the child is equipped to "pray always." First, they love learning that work can be offered as prayer, and secondly, they adapt themselves quickly to the notion that suffering is a form of prayer.

Monica, at the age of four and a half, finished her after-dinner chore one night and went in to the den to see how Jamie was coming along with his. Returning, she shook her head sadly and sighed: "Well, I guess the only people in this house who want to go to Heaven are Mommy and Daddy and me. Jamie just won't pick up the den and offer it up." And we have a small John who at two and a half, will come wailing to the house with a stubbed toe or a scraped knee and as the offended part is washed at the kitchen sink, looks up at the Crucifix over the sink and snuffles, "For you, God, for you."

At about five, most children can understand the *Our*

Father and *Hail Mary*, so we have incorporated them into the nightly prayers of the oldest, along with the *Gloria* and several personal remarks addressed to her favorite saints. At mealtime they say, "Whether we eat or sleep, whether we work or play, let it all be for the honor and glory of God." And after the meal they simply say, "Thank you, Blessed Jesus, for the lovely lunch," and ask to be excused. Grace at tables can, of course, be just about any form of address that appeals and serves it proper purpose, as long as there is some form of address used.

The morning offering is usually short, "I offer you this day as a prayer of love and thanksgiving, and I thank you for keeping me safely through the night." The "safely through the night" is not meant to imply, of course, that to die during the night would be the horror of horrors. I have heard too many Catholic mothers say, "My child says 'Now I lay me down to sleep, I pray the Lord my soul to keep,' but we leave out the 'if I should die before I wake' because I don't want my baby going to sleep with death on his mind." Of all the stages a man goes through, he has the least fear of death when he is a small child. Before he is filled with all the morbid notions adults entertain about death, death is a magical gate that leads to God and Heaven, and Heaven, of course, is wonderful. So it makes sense to a small child to be told, if He should ask, that dying in the night would be an elegant event because with God living right in his soul, it is certain he would be zipped right up to Heaven. If, however, he finds he did not die during the night, then it is quite obvious that God has work for him to do and he will thank God for keeping him to do this special work.

These prayers, which take up much more space in the writing than in the saying, cover their entire day from morning until night and they are set in a pattern which fits maturity as well as childhood. It gives them a sense of purpose in their conversations with God, supplies them with a motive for work well-done and suffering accepted, and the whole is geared to the common vocation of us, "Who are called to be saints."

CHILDREN AND CREATIVE ACTIVITY

CARYLL HOUSELANDER

If you study a diagram of the human brain you will see that almost a third of it is designed to control the movements of the hands. This ceases to surprise when you consider all that a man can do with his hands, and how different the things he does will be, according to what is in his mind.

One man will inflict a wound, another will heal one with his hands; one will strike, another will caress. There is an almost inexhaustible list of these things men do or can do with their hands, from the laying on of hands by the Bishop in confirmation to the mother's hand holding the tiny one of her small child to reassure it in the dark.

The thing I want to consider now is *making things* with the hands, especially the things that artists make, and above all what we learn from watching children making things. I say what we learn, because I am certain that we cannot *teach* children "art," but we can learn many deep, often buried, and essential things about human nature itself, and about

individual children and their needs, by watching them discover its meaning for themselves. It was through chance more
than anything else that a group of oddly assorted children
became, literally for me, the fortunes of war, and quite by
chance that I discovered from them the power to heal and
integrate that lies in art or, if you like, just in making things.
These children were refugees from Europe, very literally waifs
from the storm of war, who in most cases had lost everything, and I mean everything, not only their homes and their
country, but their sense of security, their trust in mankind,
and sometimes their own integrity. Many of them were suffering from shock, and their recent experiences had, I imag-
ined, brought to the surface symptoms of difficulties that
were there before, perhaps congenitally, but had been un-
suspected.

They came from every strata of society, from professions
and trades and business; some were the children of scaven-
gers, some were intellectual types, others natural manual la-
borers. Their ages ranged from four years old to eighteen;
but they brought younger ones to my one-room "school,"
and on one occasion, a father with a fierce black Hitler mous-
tache and the manner of a brigand—who presented himself
as "a pupil" with such insistence that it finally became necessary to form a small class of adults too.

I was supposed to teach these children, though less from
the point of view of educating them than of occupying them,
in order—since none of them fitted into the real schools—
to keep them from running wild in the streets, on which
German bombs happened to be falling with depressing regu-
larity day and night.

With the passing of the years since then, I have made
friends with many other children who in one way or another
were adrift, some from behind the Iron Curtain, some from

close at home, but who were "retarded" or "delinquent" or in some other way "maladjusted." But what I could do for these others was given to me and taught to me by that first motley crowd of refugees.

Communication

Our first difficulty was how to speak to each other. They did not speak my language, I did not speak theirs, they did not all speak each others—we were in a tower of Babel! There was only one way out, to *do*, as the cave men did, say what we wanted to by drawing pictures. After all, handwriting is only drawing countless tiny pictures of what is in your mind, and it started by the pictures the cave man drew on the walls of his cave.

Those pictures in the caves were not only messages about danger and hunger and such things; they were also, and perhaps oftener, pictures which said that the man who had made them rejoiced in the sheer vitality and beauty of the thing he drew, that in his heart there was delight in something, some animal or bird, or the shining of the sun, or an occupation of his own, like hunting, or making tools and weapons; and he could not contain this delight, he must share it with others, and the only way he could do that was to throw it outside himself, out of the wordless inward abstraction of his secret, inarticulate mind into concrete, visible form. Thus and only thus could he give shape and color to his inward joy, and so give his joy to other men.

In the earliest cave drawings we do not see merely a drawing of an animal, but of what a certain man delighted in about a particular animal.

There is nothing photogenic in these drawings, they are quite selective. Some show just the two or three long swinging lines that point to the rhythm rippling through the body

of that wild beast, others the streak of his swift flight, just
that which the artist loved, and nothing else, nothing superfluous, nothing unnecessary.

The Vague and Terrible Fears

As I have said, the earliest drawings were sometimes pictures not of what a man delighted in but of what he feared.
They might be something he feared in his own secret soul,
and which was all the more frightening because it was formless. He must, if he was to overcome it, come face to face
with it and look it squarely in the eyes, this could only be
done, in the case of a real "bogey" (an abstract thing in his
own inner consciousness), by giving it shape and form himself, so that he could look at it and, still more important, put
it under his own control.

As men developed there arose a superstition among some
of them that if a person allowed himself to be drawn he fell
into the power of the artist. To this day gypsies will refuse to
be drawn or photographed, because they believe that he who
has their image has power over them.

Children are in a sense primitive people. Every little child
is a cave man, a new man in a world which to him is new.

Nearly every child is inarticulate about that which concerns him most deeply—when he reaches an age in which
he has emotional responses to other people he is almost totally unable to express them, especially in words. About that
which causes him to suffer, and about the vague yet terrible
fears which invade him in secret, he is usually dumb.

With a young child then, art (in this case I mean drawing pictures, or making things in putty or some such substance) is as truly as it was to primitive men, a means of
communication and of *liberation*.

This I discovered very early among my refugee children,

give them paper and paint and crayons and putty and they will be able, even if you cannot (as I could not) speak their language, to tell you what is within them.

Now it is a necessity to all human beings to reveal the secrets of their soul—to express their inmost love, their secret joy, to externalize their hidden, and often unformulated fears.

To do that is the simplest and most primitive use of art.

There was one little boy who had a bogey of his own, some buried terror which, though (and largely because) he could not describe it to anyone, had made of him a mass of nerves, a victim of habits that exasperated his family, and not only anti-social to other children, but, if they ever made advances to him, positively aggressive in his self-defense. Inevitably their "advances" changed to teasing and unconscious cruelty.

This little boy began to make things with putty. At first he made potatoes and rather shapeless little animals. He never looked up while he worked, he never if he could help it, allowed anyone to see what he made, if anyone approached him while he was at work he tried to cover his little table with his body. Then one day he made his bogey. This time he did not hide it, but led me by the hand to it. There could be no possible doubt that it was meant to be a horrible thing, and certainly he had achieved that, the tiny image looked almost obscene.

The little boy looked at it with an expression of triumph, there was his bogey, that formless, colorless, nebulous horror that no one had been able to kill because no one could see it or touch it, given shape and substance, and made small enough to be crushed in *his* hand.

He had made it, it was smaller than he, it was within his power, and he could kill it!

Kill it he did, crushing it back into shapelessness and then breaking it into pieces.

It was after that that he began to play with other children.

Art Is Communion

When the artist, child or man, makes an image, not of what he fears, but of what he loves—his art is more than communication, it is *communion* with others. It is the means by which he gives the wonder of his inward self to other people, and when they respond to him by delighting in the thing he has made, it is because it also expresses that which was inarticulate in their own souls. In the thing of beauty made by a man's hands, the thing into which he has put his own life, other men recognize the secrets of their own inward lives. This is why we love old tables and chairs and such things, polished by the touch of many caressing hands, and why we want to touch them with our own hands. It is our response to the craftsman who is long dead, but whose life still comes to us in his work, our communion with someone no longer on earth, through the thing he made on earth.

A little French girl among my children made birds from scraps of felt and organdy, which were so exquisite that everyone who looked at them laughed with joy. They showed the winged, dancing quality of the child's inward life, and though they were only little pieces of material, somehow they spoke of freedom, of rising into the pure blue summer skies as effortlessly as the lark. With a trueness of instinct that was characteristic of her, this little girl brought her bright birds to the grey basement used for an air-raid shelter. It was her communion with us all, who longed for freedom and skies into which our hearts could ascend again.

One's Own Medium

I have mentioned various materials. It is important for children, for everyone, to choose their own materials. Those children in school who are restricted to one medium because it is more convenient for the teacher, are to be pitied. They will miss one of the most essential things in art—that which I call its sacramental quality.

Children should be given every kind of material that they can be given. Mud, sand, wood, paints, felt, paper, metal, water, putty and so on. God, after all, has given every substance in the world to them; He has given them seed and earth and seas and stars, shells and flowers and leaves and grass and stones and trees.

When the craftsman lays his hands upon the material into which he can most easily pour his own secret life, his touch is a caress; it is the touch of love. He will know at once that this is the substance which can receive his dream, this it is that shaped by his hands will be the shape of his shapeless longing, and will contain that which is within him and yet his heart cannot contain.

A man is never really whole until he has found that material which is for him the potential substance of his dreams. For one it will be that (to me) most beautiful of all substances, wood, wood which *lives* under the carver's hand. Another will discover his medium in earth, the rich soil that he can dig and sow and tend, until it seems to him that the spring he longed for all winter flowers from his own finger tips. Others will, like my little French girl, find woollen and cotton materials, or silk. And there are other substances to which we shall refer later, dough and flour and all the things women use to cook with, which also, through the loving contact of human hands, give tangible form to the intangible secrets of the human soul.

A Sacramental Life

People who fail completely to make any contact through their hands, with any substance that can take the shape of their thought, often become insane—or perhaps it is because they are already insane that they lack the capacity. The mind which is absolutely unable to tether its dreams to anything tangible, or to give them shape and solidity in any material, or to sow them in any solid earth, is likely to become more and more formless and to drift more and more uncontrollably into realms of unreality.

In this we have an example in a very wide sense of "Unless the seed falling into the earth die, it remaineth itself alone." Perhaps the supreme tragedy of being insane is that of being inescapably and always alone.

The reason why this contact with substance and this going out of himself into some visible substance, which he can see and touch, is so necessary to man, is because man is a sacramental creature and he is made in the likeness of God. The more closely his daily life expresses his likeness to God, the more sane, the more complete a man will be.

It is easy to see how the artist who puts his life into his clay or his wood is like God when we think of man's creation, of God taking the dust and breathing His life into it to make man.

It becomes more and more obvious when we think how Christ, the Son of God, used the humblest substances as the medium through which to give His love to men; mud and spittle on the blind man's eyes, the medium of His mercy. Writing in the dust with His finger, the medium of compassion, and for the final miracle of love, the gift of *Himself*, the simplest of all substances, bread. As if to remind us day after day that our life is by God's plan, the life of body and soul together, our supernatural life is given to us by the Church and continually renewed in us, sacramentally, through the use of the simplest substances, water, oil, salt, bread and wine.

Above all, we can see how artistic creation, approached as it should be, in humility and love, is a likeness to God, through the Incarnation.

The Word of God, the unutterable Word of the Father's love is uttered in Christ. The boundless is bound in swaddling bands, the Word is made flesh.

A Liberation

This mystery was shown to me by the experience of one boy. He was an adolescent, full of turmoil and bitterness. Every circumstance in his life had combined to twist him. He was above all afflicted by a sense of injustice and felt himself, in sheer angry self-defense, the enemy of society. If ever I have seen a human creature scourged and wounded and mocked by suffering, it was he. If ever I have seen one thrown down and crushed by the weight of the Cross, it was he. If ever I have seen one stripped naked and exposed to the misunderstanding, mockery and reproach of the world, it was he.

The material he chose to work in was wood; and like the little boy with the bogey, he worked in a corner alone, hiding his efforts. But when the work was done, it was no bogey or imp, it was a crucifix, carved crudely, yet with amazing skill. And the face, *a face of terrible suffering, was smiling!* It was the face of the young carver himself, his own features unmistakably, but transformed by that amazing smile on the face of the Crucified Christ.

The boy changed. The sudden realization of himself *indwelt by Christ*, flooded the bitterness out of him, and he became "a Christ" to the others.

The Meaning of Work

We have seen that art, making things, above all making one's own image and likeness, is a means of liberating and healing, and a means to communion. It teaches a child that basic lesson of life, the secrets of his own nature, that he is made in the likeness of God and in the pattern of Christ, and that in order to be happy through his humanity, he must live in the way that satisfies the needs, not of a cog in a machine, but of a man indwelt by God.

There is something else too, something immensely important that the child will learn from making things, this is the meaning of work, what work should be to a man or woman.

There is a common delusion that work is a punishment for sin, a hideous necessity. That it is something to be endured for the money it brings in, but a person's real life only begins when he leaves his work and seeks distraction or amusement outside it.

Yet for the average person, work takes up nearly the whole of his waking life! It is a mistake to suppose that work was intended, in the first place, to be a punishment for sin.

Work was not introduced into man's life *after* Adam sinned, but before, at the time when Adam's whole life was an uninterrupted awareness of God's presence, and his uninterrupted delight was a continual contemplation of God's goodness, beauty and love. Work was given to him as one means to that contemplation.

While the first dew still shone on the grass, the waters still trembled in the breath of the Spirit, and man's soul was as pure as the water and the dew, "...the Lord God took the man, and put him into the garden of Eden to dress it and to keep it."

Man was to know God by reflecting God's joy in creating the world, in his own soul; his work was to be a way of entering into and sharing the experience of God Himself.

He was to know the marvel of seeing the seed that had fallen from his finger tips into the earth, flowering under his feet, and to know, in so far as a finite creature can know the Infinite, the God Who made the multitudinous beauty of the world, in stars, and moon and sun, and flowers, wind and water, shadows and light, and rejoiced because He had made it. "And God saw everything that he had made, and behold it was very good."

No Easy Creation

That which *did* follow on sin, as part of man's punishment was that his work was to become a painful effort to him. He was no longer able to make anything with the ease of a creator, no longer would beauty overflow from his heart spontaneously and pour from his hands, flooding the world with its life—no, now he must wrestle with nature, and the substances he would work in would not yield to him unless he literally strove with them in the sweat of his brow.

"In the sweat of thy face shalt thou eat bread, til thou return into the ground."

But Christ, Himself working in the sweat of His face, restored even this aspect of work to its glory, making it again a constant act of adoration.

The artist, and I count a good craftsman as an artist, knows the cost of acquiring skill; it is only those who do approach their work with the artist's attitude who will go through the necessary years of daily effort, practice and patience. To become a skilled craftsman means imposing upon oneself the discipline that forms character.

It would be impossible, for example, for an impatient, careless man to become a skilled woodworker. The uninitiated watching a carpenter at work suppose it easy—and indeed nothing is more lovely than to watch the apparent ease with which he planes and cuts and fits his wood. The rhythmic, swinging movements of his arms, the long easy sweep of his plane, the shavings falling away lightly curled and thin as rose petals. And then the exactitude with which the pieces fit together and interlock, and all the time the man's obvious pride and pleasure in his work.

Yes, it looks easy, and it has become easy too for the master craftsman, but what long self-discipline has produced that ease in him, that precision and lightness of touch, that flowing movement, and what constant application has enabled him to sharpen and set his tools to cut clean and to know his different woods, with their special grains, and even their special moods!

It is this apprenticeship that restores man's pride and dignity in work and fits him to do the work that makes his own soul luminous in the shadow of the Trinity.

Now if we turn back to the diagram of the brain and study it again, remembering the reasons why it is a need of man's nature to co-ordinate hands and mind, it no longer seems strange at all that so much of the brain has been made for that very purpose. But if we turn from this study to the study of our contemporary society, we cannot be surprised by the prevalent discontent, joylessness and lack of direction or purpose that is its depressing characteristic.

Co-ordinating Minds and Hands

How many people today ever use their hands intelligently?—indeed how many there are who practically never use them at all!

Above all how many are there whose daily work means making something conceived in their own minds?

Again how many are there who can *choose* the work they are to do all their lives? And among the few who can choose, how many are there in whom the artist has not been destroyed, so that ignorant of their real needs they are often rejecting their true happiness by their choice?

Girls and boys go into factories at sixteen, or into shops or offices or one of the professions a year or two later. In the factories most people make, not a whole thing they want to, but part of something they probably never see whole.

Most people are working simply for the money they have to earn, and they only start to live when the day's work ends, and even then few start to live in any full sense, for most people go in search of machine-made entertainment and canned emotion.

When I think of these sad multitudes, I am reminded of those children who are"backward" or "maladjusted," who so often have very poor co-ordination between their hands and their minds. The workers of the world today seem to me very like those children, they seem to have lost that co-ordination. I believe the only remedy for the tragedy of our industrial civilization is to restore it.

My theory is grounded in the belief that every human being is an artist, simply because he is made in God's image and indwelt by His spirit.

The artist has been submerged in most men, but because it is his true nature, it can always be restored.

The Artist in the Child

Again, I think of the backward children and of one in particular who, because she was regarded as "hopeless," typifies the sad multitude.

This child lived in a slum. She came regularly to a little group of children to whom I gave materials to work in, and she watched them working. Because her hands were so clumsy she was a source of irritation to her own family and was shunned by other children. She dropped things, broke things, she ate dirtily, she could not tie bows or fasten buttons. She was retarded, and utterly incapable of speaking about what was in her mind. I need not add that she was a very discouraged child, already accepting herself as being useless, even despicable.

Yet she came to the group, fascinated by watching them, pathetically longing to do something like they did. She hovered on the outskirts, going round behind the chairs of the workers, staring.

When the others had gone and I was mopping up the inevitable mess, this child stayed behind with me, usually watching with a faint pitiful smile.

One night she very gingerly took a rag and mopped up too. Then she did it night after night and came to do it well. From that time she began to have self-respect. Very slowly, very painfully she learned, by copying my hands, to tie bows, to fasten buttons, and crowning triumph, to brush and part her hair!

And one day she sat down at the table with the others and began to make things with plasticene.

I have seen many other children learn this co-ordination of head and hands in just this slow painful way, and with just this growing self-respect and happiness. Craftsmen acquiring their skill.

If *they* can restore the artist in themselves, so also can the adults of the world, but the adults, like the children, will only realize what it is that they lack and want if they *see* artists at work.

Artists are considered in these days to be something like freaks; "practical" people who do not realize that they are repressed artists themselves, mistrust them, and feel that they need some excuse, some justification for being artists. They are usually poor and, in the world's eyes, improvident, because for the sheer joy of their work they are content to remain poor.

If they do need a justification, they have one; it is that they show the world what every man's work should be like. It should be his joy. Moreover, they show what every man's work would be like had not the artist in him been stifled.

I do not think it over-optimistic to say that if the majority of men really saw the ideal of work, and wanted it, they would bring about a bloodless revolution. For whatever men *really* want they always get. When they want higher wages, they strike for them, when they want shorter hours, they strike for them, when they want better material conditions they strike for them—and they get them.

If the day comes when men strike for creative work, work that means contemplation and restores the worker to his glory—they will get happiness.

The first step in bringing that about is, don't destroy the artist in the child; every child is a poet until he is ten, and every child, so long as he is not taught, can draw and model until he is ten. But too many teachers destroy the poet and the artist in the child.

Art is regarded in many schools and homes as a luxury, a graceful but unnecessary accomplishment, or a hobby for leisure.

Thus it is divorced from life.

Too often art teachers impose their own ideas upon children; one sees whole pathetic classes struggling to draw, say a flower in an earthenware pot, with a lead pencil, to please a teacher who is as bored as they are. In these children the artist withers.

Not for After-hours

Art is a sacramental thing, it is a welding together and
fusing together of spirit and matter, and the matter may be
anything from glass to mud.

Art is not a hobby. Those who try to compensate for the
soul-lessness of their work by using arts and crafts as a hobby
outside working hours simply underline and condone the
failure of our civilization.

What we need is to bring to whatever work we do the
attitude of the artist, and if there is any kind of work that
makes this *impossible*, choose not to do that kind—but make
no mistake, in order to be an artist in work it is not necessary
to be a painter or a sculptor or a specialist in any "fine art."

It makes no difference how seemingly humble the work
is, it may be kneading a piece of dough to make a loaf, or
mixing the flour to make a pie. It may be dusting or scrubbing, or polishing a chair or table, as well as making one. It
may be sewing a dress or making a toy for a child.

The thing that matters is that what we do is something
we do with a strong desire to do it, and strong enough love at
the core of it to make it worth while to acquire the skill, and
to do it with the loving care and pride and joy of the skilled
worker, and that into the work we put our own life. We
must take hold of the ordinary things of the earth, and what
is in our hearts must flow into them through the caressing
touch of our hands.

It may not always be apparent even that we are making a
thing, a work of art, for many of the things we do make
every day are impermanent; the pie that is eaten, the little
dress soon outgrown, the flower sown to bloom and wither
so swiftly!

But the fact remains that with the substance of these
passing things, and if we have it with the vision that is in a

child's soul, we are making home, we are making happiness, we are making love, and through our daily work turned to contemplation, each one of us will know the secret splendor of "The Word is made flesh" in his own life.

READING THE OLD TESTAMENT

MARY REED NEWLAND

Probably the reason people do not read Scripture to their children is that they do not read it to themselves. At least that is why I didn't, when I didn't. And why I do, now that I do. Probably another reason why they don't read it to their children is they are afraid of it.

"You don't mean to tell me you read the Old Testament to your small children and they understand!" When I said yes, I do, and they love it, this young mother trotted home with doubts, tried it, and *her* children loved it. And since this is to be a short article, the best way I know of scouting all the apprehensions of mothers and fathers who have them on this score, is to say, "Try it—you'll see," and add a few things we have discovered that help along the way.

There is, I think, an important difference between reading from Scripture and reading "Bible stories," even from the excellent editions of Bible stories now available. We have several of the latter, beautifully done with handsome illustrations, and our children never get enough of them—but we still read to them from the Bible itself. Because the whole object of reading from the Bible is to convince them these stories are really found there, can be highly entertaining and inspiring, and to pave the way to the day when they will want to follow our example and read it for themselves.

Adapting the Bible for Children

The first thing to understand is that you cannot read the Old Testament to children verbatim. Some of the new translations have passages which do make great sense as they stand, but usually you have to strip the words down to their age level and vocabulary. What it amounts to is a kind of story-telling after all, but with the book there to prompt you. It must be a "reading" to them, even if you merely skim the text with your eye, improvise and ad lib large parts of it. It helps those who can read, and do—over your shoulder—to see how one can transcribe the involved passages with their repetitions and intricate wording to make very modern sounding tales. Not that you remove them from their setting in antiquity, that would be wrong, but if you read them to children in their own language they are better able to see for themselves the similarity between men and their behavior several thousand years ago, and men and their behavior now. Whether they know it or not, they will begin to grow in the understanding that there is nothing new under the sun, and that sin and sanctity have always been a matter of one's rebellion against, or love for, God.

Keep It Interesting

It is important to read ahead of time whatever story you have chosen, for a number of reasons all of which you will discover fast enough if you dive in without any preparation.

First, because children are bored with too much repetition, with too many difficult names and family trees. If they are important to the story you can pare them down and use what is important, but leave the rest out. An example of this is the introduction to Mordechai, in the second chapter, fifth verse of the Book of Esther. He is called "the son of Jair, the son of Semei, the son of Cis, of the race of Jemini who had been carried away from Jerusalem at the time that Nebechenezzor (same thing as Nabuchodonosor), king of Babylon, carried away Jechonias, king of Juda." If the children know the story of Daniel, what this means is that Mordechai was a descendant of those Jews carried off by Nebechenezzor, among whom was Daniel and the three youths of fiery furnace fame; maybe Mordechai was even some kind of buttonhole great-grand-cousin to Daniel. So it helps spark Mordechai's characterization to use this. Knowing who was his father, grandfather and great-grandfather leaves them cold and they will sit politely stone deaf until all that is over.

What About the Hot Passages?

Next there are passages from the Old Testament which read more like pages out of the *American Medical Journal* or *True Confessions* than Holy Writ, and stumbling onto these unprepared will involve you in some mighty touchy discussions of anatomy and the sins of the flesh. So one must be cued to skipping them ahead of time. The Book of Esther provides more examples—but at the same time is an exciting story which all children love. For instance, all those eunuchs around the palace, guarding gates, plotting, having charge over the concubines (horrors—what to do about concubines?). Needless to say, we do not go into the business of eunuchs and concubines, but translate them as "servants" and "er—sort of like wives," explaining that in those days it was sometimes the custom to have more than one wife. The word virgin is used often, with undertones that indicate something very specific, so we translate it as a young maiden who was pure and good and had not married, and make very sure they do not attach to its frequent use the same gifts of holiness as were Our Lady's.

Then there is King Assuerus' habit of entertaining at banquets and ending up, after much drinking of wine, "well-warmed and merry." It suffices to say the king was feeling rather jolly, and the children are content.

There's that short passage (again in Esther, but do not think these things are peculiar to this Book alone—they appear all over the place) about the maidens competing for role as queen, going in to see the king in the evening and coming out in the morning, and if they did not please him going off to the palace of the concubines. We omit this one entirely. And toward the end of the story there is Aman's eleventh-hour attempt to save his neck by seducing the queen, while the king is out in his "garden set with trees" collecting his wits. There is little left to conjecture in this passage so we improvise, and translate the lines about the king's return, his accusation: "The king was *wild!*" And when it goes on to say, "The word was not yet gone out of the king's mouth and immediately they covered his (Aman's) face," we read: "Before the king was even finished yelling at Aman, they popped a bag over his head." This is a great moment for all and the story breaks up momentarily while all the small boys present pop bags over each other's heads.

It is also important to read the footnotes ahead of time, so there need be no time out for investigating fine print. For instance, in the Book of Daniel it tells of Daniel and his friends refusing to eat the fine palace fare, but asking per-

mission to have "pulse" instead. Pulse, the footnote tells, is "peas, beans, and such like." This is a good place to stop and discuss the merits of fasting and its spiritual rewards because Daniel and the youths looked finer and fairer after their fast than the others after their eating. And God rewarded Daniel with great gifts of grace after his fasting. In the story of David, too, there is mention of "frumenty," which is not explained in the footnotes but should be looked up in the dictionary. It is defined as "a pudding made of hulled wheat." All these things help to make the story warm and folksy and the children like to stop and compare them with the things they eat. It also helps to get such things as pea soup and baked beans, hot oatmeal, down them cheerfully when they are inclined to whine about eating their meals.

Skip the Long Prayers

Another thing one must be prepared to omit, regretfully, are the long prayers. When children want a story, they want action—not a doxology. They will grow up to love the prayers, but most of the time are bored if you insist on breaking up a good story to read them. It is enough to say, "And then they said a lovely prayer about how good God was to them, and they thanked Him very much."

I was forced to surrender on the matter of long prayers when reading the story of the three youths in the fiery furnace, from Daniel. The children had used their own version of this Canticle for processions in the pasture in summer, but in the middle of this story all they wanted to know was whether the youths got out of the furnace—and trying to read the prayer was a total failure. John settled down to pulling his jersey up over his nose, Jamie to shredding the tobacco out of someone's stale cigarette, and Peter quietly to poking holes in the couch with a pencil. All these things indicate one thing solely—perfect and complete boredom. So we mentally blue-pencil the Canticle now and jump to the 91st verse (third chapter): "Then Nebechenezzor, the king, was amazed and jumped up right off his throne and said to his nobles, 'Good grief, didn't we throw three men tied hand and foot into the middle of that fire?' And they answered, 'We certainly did, O king.' And he said: 'Well, I see four men now, loose and walking around in the fire and not a blister on them, and the fourth looks like the Son of God.'"

Jamie says: "Boy!"

John yells: "A miracle!"

And *that's* the reaction you want when you read your children the Old Testament. Hopalong was never like this. There is more good red blood spilled in these stories than in all the westerns from now to doomsday and it's all *true*. It's all told in terms of good and evil, with God the most important character of all, and if you read it well and moralize in a nice way as you go along (not too long-winded) they get the point and agree heartily.

Don't Sound Bible-ish

One more thing is important and that is not to intone these stories, or give them your best in the flute-like voice department. If you are going to sound Bible-ish, they won't come running back for more very often. Really let go when you read, get excited, stick in little asides that help point up the humor, stop and encourage short discussions and especially make much of the small but endearing details.

Our Mother's Club, which meets monthly, did a session on reading the Old Testament to children and we recommend it as a good practice run for mothers who would like to try and are a little self-conscious. Each mother brought her own Bible and we took turns reading the story of Daniel aloud, improvising the way we would for children. Most of us were reading it for the first time and it took us no time at all to get the knack. One mother for instance translated Nebechenezzor's rebuke to his wise men (called to tell him his dream) as, "You're *stalling*." Everyone whooped and hollered at this—it was such a perfect choice of word.

The Story of Esther

Perhaps we should go back to the story of Esther, for those who don't know it, and assure them it is not all delicate situations. There are wonderful accounts of the way the king decorated his palace for his banquets, and gave instructions at one of them that no one need drink or eat anything they didn't want. O boy—you could leave stuff on your plate and no one said a word. There are yards and yards of beautiful clothes and jewels for the maidens to wear, and knowing well how ladies dawdle over their dressing, the king gave all the competing maidens *twelve months* to get ready for the Queen Contest.

There is one passage in the beginning especially pertinent to wives. Queen Vashti is dethroned for disobedience to her husband, and when the king asked his wise men what sort of punishment should be prescribed, Manuchen, the chief counsellor, gave a thought-provoking answer. Not only had she done a bad thing by her disobedience, said he, but if she were allowed to get away with it she would go about laughing at the king behind his back and soon the gossip of it all over the kingdom would have wives everywhere "despising their husbands." So he advised the king to write a letter for all the realm, reminding all that husbands are to be "masters in their own households."

Then there is Esther's plan for saving the Jews after Aman had manoeuvered their death warrant. Did she dash into the throne room weeping and wailing in sackcloth and ashes? No indeed. The way to a man's heart is through his stomach, so she put on her royal apparel, went before the king and invited him and Aman to a banquet. Not until the king was feeling quite jolly (well-warmed, etc.) did she tell him (this is at a *second* banquet) that Aman, the wretch, had plans to put her and her people to death. And Aman was duly escorted to the gibbet he had raised to hang Mordechai, and was hanged until he was dead. Hurray. Mordechai—Esther's uncle, incidentally—emerged triumphant, wearing garments of sky color and violet and wearing the king's own ring (which the king had the foresight to remove from Aman's finger before he was hanged) and promoted to position of overseer over the Queen's household....

Reading Bears Fruit

Reading the Old Testament to children teaches them many things. It probes far back to the roots of our own Liturgy. It follows the course of events from the fall to the coming of Christ at Bethlehem and prophesies His glorious resurrection on Easter. It draws the whole plan of the redemption for them and begins to illuminate the prayers of the Mass. And together with the lives of the martyrs and saints of the New Testament, it gives them the best answer of all to the widespread proposition that men and women who love God in the heroic manner are sissies and cannot compete with cowboys and space cadets today.

There it is, part of the most exciting book on earth, and so many of us never open it. We cheat ourselves and our children of our richest heritage when we don't.

RECREATION AND CHILDREN

MARY REED NEWLAND

Recreation means so many different things to so many people that this trying to sit down and write simply about "recreation" is likely to end up way off center. For some people it means what you do at summer camp, summer resorts, or clam bakes. And for some it means what you do on playgrounds, at nursery schools or on nature walks. And for still some more it means deciding between the movies, TV, dinner and dancing or a drink with friends, and so on. One man's meat is another man's poison and to try to describe recreation as everyone sees it is impossible.

It Must Be Fun

For parents, recreation is as much a part of the spiritual training of their children as anything else, with one simple distinction: to be recreation, for a child, it must be fun. The other lessons aren't always fun, and some can be quite painful, but this one doesn't qualify unless it is. It isn't always fun for mothers, and in their human weakness, at the end of a long day of interruptions and messes and wasted time, they are likely to look at some of the most satisfying forms of recreation and see them as strictly a pain in the neck. By the same token, a child will sometimes look back on what parents have planned as a recreation and be either too tired, too full, too confused to get much benefit from it. This is not meant to be, however, a blanket disapproval of planned recreation or a finger-wagging at mothers who can't take mud pies on the kitchen floor, but simply a reflection on the fact that recreation thinking these days has taken such a specialized turn that we are inclined to lose our really delicate perception in regard to it.

The first years of a child's life are almost all recreation, or he won't get through them happily. From his point of view and for all he doesn't know it, learning, eating, discovering, inventing, all things that are fun and exciting, even humdrum but satisfying, are a form of recreation, which the dictionary defines as "refreshment of body or mind; diversion, amusement, as a pleasurable exercise or occupation." And the best clues to what recreation is for him comes from him. Toys come first of all, at least things to play with, and here he often neatly evades what the grown-ups would have him accept as proper and fitting things. For example, take every family's experience with the baby who, having unveiled all the Christmas gifts, returns to the kitchen to get out the pots and pans on Christmas morning. After talking a lot but doing nothing about it, this past Christmas we bought our baby's gifts in the housewares department of the five and ten and he had the best time ever with sets of colored paper cups, plastic measuring spoons, a plastic scratcher for scrubbing pots and pans and a slightly off-plumb egg beater. Not that he did not enjoy the gifts other people gave him, but children have an affinity for imitating grown-ups in their play and to take advantage of it is to open one of the widest corridors to a child's learning.

Work Is Play

Little girls love getting toy dishes and stoves, but they prefer being busy around their mothers' dishes and stoves and until they grow wary enough to identify such carryings on with work (and, absorbing some of the attitude of a fallen world toward work, start to shy away from it) some of their very best times are had wiping dishes, overseeing the cooking, and especially, particular joy, scrubbing the sink. They sometimes waste more scouring powder than they need, and hypnotized by the multiplication of soapsuds, pour out more soap than they need, but the meditations and musings to be bought for a nickel's worth of soap or scouring powder are rare and wonderful things, and if we really stopped to put a value on them we'd find such soul-satisfactions cannot be bought for a price. One of the most confounding evidences for the argument that recreation is sometimes intimately allied to forms of work is that remark often heard from little girls, "I love doing dishes at someone else's house."

So just because a kitchen is associated in our minds as a place to work does not mean that it is not one of the very best places to play, also. Just as garages and cellar work benches are, for little boys, very good places to play. If we have lost sight of this, not because we are stupid or insensitive but merely busy and distracted, we can regain the perspective by stopping to put ourselves in their places, to see, not the work schedule interrupted by the pottering child, but the pottering child who will soon be a woman. Considering the span from the cradle to the grave and the reason for man's being here, play that is imitation of man's work is really instinctive, and understandable, and God's way for preparing His creatures little by little for maturity. And it shows that God made man so that no matter how rich or how poor, recreation depends more on what is inside him than what is outside, and why, when to his parents the cluttered yard and the bald spots on the lawn are anathema, to a child they can be a paradise.

Sometimes it is the children of the poor who invent the best recreations of all, precisely because they must invent them. Once, when we were really scraping the bottom of the barrel, we discovered our boys—with nothing that would qualify remotely as commonly catalogued recreational paraphernalia—had taken an old mop handle, fastened to it a piece of discarded hose, dragged alongside an empty crate and on the crate was the sad, sad, remnant of what had once been another child's toy tractor. One boy was in the crate, under the tractor, giving it a grease job, and another was pumping gas in it with the hose fastened to the mop handle. If we had qualms about what a child needs to be provided with in order to entertain and instruct himself, it was then we cast them to the winds.

Educational Toys

It's so much simpler than the specialists like to imply. We know of a couple who were determined their child should have nothing but the most highly recommended educational toys to play with—which toys are good and fun, but along with them goes a kind of informal I.Q. test. They bought a wooden mailbox equipped with different shaped blocks which fitted into shaped slots, and presenting it, sat back to calculate their small son's ability to figure out which blocks went into which slots. He looked it over, took out all the blocks, then turning the box upside down discovered the master slot for removing the blocks, opened it and willy-nilly, dumped in the blocks. God love him, he was so far ahead of them that one encounter left it behind—for all it was prescribed for his age and development.

So recreation, it seems, is a very fluid thing and likely to be discovered under the appearances of mere meddling, or messing around, or cluttering up, and is also sometimes quite recognizable as "play." Like all other things in life, it has to be subject to some regulation but at the same time not categorized and frozen in a set form. No one is suggesting, of course, that all a child's recreational peccadilloes be catered to or tolerated *ad infinitum* for fear of cutting him off from his play—or, like one family, the jungle gym be moved into the living room (it really happened) come winter and the end of the climbing outdoors season. It simply takes the same love and judgment (how easy this sounds!) to handle it as it takes to handle rewards, punishments, assignment of work,

and all the rest of the parts of growing up. And like these other things, it has a definite relation to God and along with "recreating" should go learning to offer it to God.

Recreation and Religion

"You mean," Peter said, "that you can offer everything that's good to God? Playing? Even just standing still?" Even playing, just standing still, everything that is good, because everything that is good is a reflection of God's goodness and is a gift as much as those strange gifts of pain and trial He sends to perfect our wills. We receive the grace to have fun, just as we receive the grace to do other things. And if we remind them often enough and lovingly enough, and after really good fun, perhaps we shall help establish the connection between all forms of recreation and prayer. Otherwise, unless one anticipates a life of endless misery, it would be impossible to "pray always." At the same time it ought to establish deep in the subconscious, the instinctive awareness of things that are fitting recreation as compared to those which are not fitting, and therefore cannot be offered as prayer.

There is a disinclination on the part of some people to "drag religion" into the business of having fun, when to ignore our relation to God in our recreation (while bleating constantly to Him about our work, our finances, our aches and pains) is the thing that is out of place, not the reverse. I have never seen a picnic or a beach party spoiled yet by the acknowledgment, "Wasn't God good to give us this lovely day," or "If it weren't for original sin, there'd be no sand in the potato salad," and barring overdoses of out and out sermons, the fabric of detachment—seeing all things against a background of God—is woven step by step a little bit tighter with each acknowledgment that, but for His cloudless sky, or warm sand, or infinite foresight that would permit man to one day invent the hot dog, this party wouldn't have been half as much fun.

And at the times of the great feasts, outright religious recreations, including even mixed groups, are far more successful and satisfying—by virtue of the graces of the feasts, I am sure—than amusement for the sake of amusement. Many times it is the only opportunity for apparently religion-less people to acknowledge, awkwardly perhaps, a divine instinct deep inside which wants to be given a voice. The times when we have invited non-Catholics to celebrate the great vigils or feasts with us have been very happy gatherings, with—in the case of Halloween—the interesting discovery that when the background for the vigil is explained, the compulsion to indulge in even mild vandalism seems pointless.

Community Recreation

Because we are part of society, it is important that we think of recreation in terms of neighborhood and community recreation as well as in terms of family recreation. I know no parents who are deliberately anticipating bad entertainment habits as part of their children's growing up—only those who worry about the possibility; but too often all thought on the subject omits any real practical effort to forestall what is undesirable. It isn't an original idea, but neighborhood action is the answer and recently several nationally circulated articles have told of communities enforcing curfews, party conventions, formal dress customs and so forth. Most of these accounts have dealt with situations already out of hand, and how they were brought under control, but what is to stop the parents of the very young from establishing patterns which will preclude their getting out of hand?

We have begun feeling our way with a plan in our neighborhood and even though there is wide difference in our various religious beliefs, we all agree that we want to raise wholesome, moral children.

Mountain Climbing

Our initial step at a neighborhood entertainment was a mountain climb. We have on our land what is (by some people) laughingly called a "mountain" complete with trees, rocks, lichen, moss, fungi, birds, animals and fresh air. Best of all, it has a top which, when you reach it, you sit on and then you turn around and come down. Children from four to ten years old were included, with five mothers—we had twenty people in all. We all climbed, and after the climb we all ate, informally, coffee cake and cocoa. Not very world-shaking, but highly successful as a planned recreation and the goodbyes were studded with, "Oh thanks—we had the *best* time." Living with a mountain ceases to be a novelty after a while, and under other circumstances I might have heard my children react to the suggestion that they climb it with, "Oh, mother—we already *climbed* it." But gather a group of people together and suggest it, and all of a sudden it's a terrific idea. So too is eating your lunch, or picking blueberries, or wading in the brook—when you all do it together. We haven't the time or money or transportation facilities to go off on elaborate forays in search of recreation, but we can work away at the business of establishing in our children's minds many wholesome forms of recreation by planning the simple things, and getting them to do them together.

Successful group recreation doesn't seem to depend on the elaborate as much as it does on unity and enthusiasm, and if our experiences have been a measure, I think that city families in the same block or apartment house can make trips to the park, to the zoo, rides on the ferry, a trip to the museum just as exciting for their children as our (really prosaic) mountain climb was for ours, without spending more than bus fare or money for ice cream cones.

Families Can Recreate Together

What's new about all this? Nothing—really, except perhaps our stopping to observe that more and more we have grown used to the idea that planned recreation is the function of recreation directors, community centers, summer playground programs, day camps and scout troops. And if we are convinced that this is so, then we have been sold a bill of goods. Somehow, some way, families—even families with one or two babies still in diapers, and fathers working odd shifts in factories—can challenge this idea that recreation for all of them together is no longer possible. If no other way, then by doing as a family I know did—declaring Thursday "children's day" and leaving the chores where they were at a set time and simply doing things that were fun together. To neglect recreation, to consign it to the category of things "kids will do anyway," is like saying "kids will eat anyway," and not bothering to care what they eat.

And looking ahead to the day when in high school, they will be driven by that overpowering urge to run with the pack—to neglect the opportunities to band together now in neighborhood groups and plan wholesome recreation is missing the one big chance to set the standards of the pack. Groups of Catholic high school girls all over the country have begun to establish conventions in modest evening dresses simply by, together, demanding them from designers. Whether it's strapless evening dresses, driving cars, drinking, whatever, something *can* be done and the earlier the better. Small children gather the strength and security for sound social behavior first of all from their spiritual training and their family life, but sometimes the best of them alone will waver before the pressure of ridicule and custom and "everybody does it." Supported by a group whose tastes are as wholesome as theirs, they stand a much better chance of weathering the delicate, dangerous years of adolescence and first experiments with maturity.

A Community Fair

Through organizations like PTA and others, essentially family organizations, there is recreational application to be made on even a broader level—the community itself. Our PTA is holding a Town Fair this year, the first in many years, and almost the entire program depends on the fruits of creative family recreation, whether crafts, hobbies, flowers, herbs, art work or whatever. And for all the fun of entering the exhibits, the best fun of all is going together, with the mothers stopping to see the quilts and hooked rugs and the needlepoint, and the fathers the cabinet work and the metal craft and the chair caning, and the children to smell the herbs—taste them if they are brave, and discuss the flower show awards, criticize the art. Hard work, you may say, putting on a fair—hardly a recreation for any but those who will stroll through it. But not many of the people who work on it would agree. It is hard work, but in a strange way it is also recreation.

Re-creating Gladness

Defining recreation gets "curiouser and curiouser" as you try to track the meaning down, because it is so many different things to so many different people. For some it is work, for some play, for some study, for one lady I know it is caring for the altar and cleaning the sanctuary (most of her friends tell her this is a job for the janitor). Maybe the reason it is so elusive is that we never really look at the word and what it's made of—re-creation. What man attempts to do when he seeks recreation as a change and a refreshment from the weariness of his daily work is to re-create the gladness of heart of his first parents before the fall, when all the world and all of life was full of joy in a creation that was free of sin. Christ accomplished a re-creation when He redeemed us and poured

His blood over a fallen world, establishing a society in His Mystical Body through which we could find paradise again in spite of the continuing presence of evil.

Outside of Him, all our attempts to recreate fall short, the joy is never more than transitory, the recreation rarely more than a diversion. But in Him we can find it—and maybe that is the secret of why the saints' lives were such a fusion of what we call by the common words—work, suffering, prayer, play—because they discovered that He is the instrument of re-creation, and in Him all human activity can become a recreation.

PROGRESSIVE EDUCATION

SR. ST. FRANCIS, S.S.J.

By dint of thought, profound and deep,
With worry sore, and loss of sleep,
We now produce a college grad
Who cannot write or spell or add;
Whose reading's immature as yet;
Who doesn't know the alaphabet.
Although the superstructure's splendid,
The thing's not quite what we intended;
For somehow, we, in our elation,
Forgot to put in the foundation.

CHILDREN–AND THE IMITATION OF MARY

MARY REED NEWLAND

There is probably no woman who ever lived more maligned at the hands of her admirers than the Mother of God. Out of the endless reservoir of her virtues, her wisdom, her beauty of body and soul, there has emerged a nightmarish parade of Marys, and more arty rubbish, trashy verse, and pure sugar has been spun in her praise than one has the heart or the head to calculate. That some of it is sincere and, in that light praiseworthy, need not be gone into here since the point of this piece is not to walk the tightrope between art and sincerity; but at least it can be said that even in the case of the praiseworthy frights created in her name, the effect can be, and often is, devastating. And as though it weren't bad enough to have so much trash about masquerading as tribute, the greatest devastation of all is the complete obliteration, for so many, of the real magnificence behind the saccharine curtain. The whole mess has a yeasty quality—left alone, in the warm temperature of a well-disposed imagination, it begins to work like a dough, growing and spreading until finally it fills the vessel and there is no room for more. And when it is the mind of a child that is filled, then the pity is double, because the transcending personality of the Mother of God, who should be the companion of their growing up, their model of virtue, their source of all grace, is reduced to nothing but confection treading pearly clouds and strangling in blue chiffon. She will serve them as a pretty distraction in their infancy, compel them to an outward display of Christian manners in their early school years, but when the chips are down and passion and temptation are to be faced, at last, her substance is that of a creature in a pretty dream, the last woman under the sun to face, much less tackle, the problems that go hand in hand with human weakness.

Children Need Mary

Children need Mary from the very beginning. They need her when they are beginning to wake up to the world around them, to their place in it, to their bodies—so alive with interest and stimulation, pain and pleasure. And children want her. They want her because deep inside of every man is the desire to be loved and understood by someone whose devotion is unchanging and whose judgments are ever just. Human mothers are not paragons of virtue, unless and until, with grace, in that last final gasp they reach sanctity. And for all the tenacity of a small child's devotion to his mother, it is only a matter of time before he is forced to admit that mother is neither infallible nor impeccable. But Mary is.

The problem is not, primarily, to convince the Catholic parent that if we are to lead our children to Christ, we must lead them through Mary—that is pretty commonly understood. But the big struggle seems to lie in giving Mary to children in a form that is sustaining all through the years of their early childhood, up to and beyond adolescence, and into the years of a growing maturity—with the relationship between the child and Mary growing, not diminishing.

Perhaps the weak spot is this predilection for the Mary of the apparitions, to the neglect of the Mary of Nazareth. Not that the antidote for the distortion of Mary is a neglect of Our Lady of Lourdes, or Guadalupe, or La Salette, or Fatima, but the Mary of the apparitions totally divorced from her life on this earth is incomplete, too, and not so much in danger of neglect as the former, but in danger of being transformed into something bordering on the superstitious. Or perhaps the trouble is the contrast between the abundant detail of the apparitions, and the scarcity of it in her life in the gospels. Her heroism is there, in the gospels, but it is told with such understatement that it takes digging and thinking and meditating to find it, and we are too lazy to do that when we can pick up holy cards and take someone else's word for what she was like. But it is the Mary of the gospels we must give our children to imitate, who once lived in the world they live in, and who served God perfectly in it.

Mary's Love for God

Mary served God perfectly because first of all she loved Him perfectly, and the first step in the imitation of Mary is to love God. It is no good to recommend Mary as, say, a model of humility if one does not know that it was out of love there grew humility. Without first love, and then the humility, the *Magnificat* would be consummate pride.

Without the love, there would have been no heroic courage, and without the courage, no *Fiat*. Hers was an intimate knowledge of Scripture and the Prophets, and it was no mystery to Mary what end lay in store for the Messias. Perhaps the details were lacking, still hidden in the mind of God, but the end of it all had been familiar to her ever since she had learned to read. And yet at the age of fifteen, she had the courage to face the prospect of inevitable anguish and say, "Be it done unto me according to Thy word."

Imitating Her Purity

Then there is purity, another virtue children must be urged to imitate in Mary. Mary's was a rare and wonderful purity, and based—if we are to read the account of the Annunciation correctly—on a full knowledge of how the body functions. Gabriel told her she was to be the mother of a child—and she did not ponder it silently, but asked immediately: "How shall this be done, because I know not man?" I would be willing to wager that a picture of the fifteen-year-old Mary, dazzling as she was in her array of graces, virtues, talents, attributes, all the rest—but also with an orderly knowledge of sex and its functions, would leave many a pious Catholic in a state of deep shock. It shouldn't—there were no gaps in the glory she wove for God; it was a fabric made of her whole being, both her body and her soul, and in the perfect knowledge and ordering of the body's functions there is a giving of glory to God. More than anyone who ever lived, she gave Him glory—ignorance was not part of it. And yet we have vast numbers of parents who persist in the notion that Mary's chastity consists, *in toto*, of a kind of superficial modesty.

Imitation of Mary's chastity is premised first of all on knowing what chastity is, and if it is a denial, of what it is a denial. It seems to occur to very few that chastity is, in the first place, not a denial of anything—that it is a positive state, and not a negative. In the second place, it is a denial—but in the first, it is a giving. Chastity is not a sour apple. It is the full, ripe, beautiful fruit plucked and given to God. In the sense that, given to God, it cannot be consumed by one's self—then it is denial, but who defines the giving of gifts to a lover as denial? These things are the privileges that go with being in love, and Mary's chastity was, again, not a denial of her own full, capable, fertile humanity, but a giving of this to God because in her love she would hold back nothing.

No Silly Stuff

Obedience is another of her virtues that flows from her love of God. This is what parents overlook. This is the thing they so often miss when pressing the Mary-virtues on their young—both their young young and their older young. One is not virtuous for the sake of being virtuous, or else it is not virtue. One is virtuous for the love of God.

This is a revolutionary idea—at least when applied to the theory that the imitation of Our Lady begins and ends in acting like a lady. It is the enemy of all the sentimental nonsense which results in an over-elaborate piousness with pictures, holy cards, statues and the like. I shall never forget the account of a school piano recital given to me by a sweet, pious child of twelve.

"Oh dear," she said, "Was I ever in a mess! A card slipped out of my music book. I had to keep playing with one hand, lean over and pick up the card with the other, and then of course because it was a holy card, I had to kiss it before I put it back in my book."

I am not saying that the Blessed Mother was not touched by this sincere act of devotion on the part of a loving child. It is not that she would kiss the holy card that is wrong—it is that she is afraid not to kiss it, and I may sound extremely sour, but this sort of thing leads many times, either directly or indirectly, to apostasy.

Far more healthy is the remark from an eight-year-old not long ago: "You know—I just don't like the pictures they make of the Blessed Mother." Pictures, in her mind, are pictures—and one is free to like or dislike them without any fear of dishonoring Mary. Pictures, manners, the length of her skirt, the face without make-up, the nails without polish, are not the substance of imitation of Mary. That, as has been said but cannot be said often enough, lies first of all in loving God.

Imitating Her Love

Teaching a small child to love God is incredibly easy because God does so much of the work Himself. In baptismal splendor, the soul is free of any impediment, is the dwelling of the Holy Trinity, and is awaiting the pouring in of revelation. With the knowledge that there is a God, that He loves and wants to be loved, and if we ask, He will teach us to love—with this, spiritual activity begins. We can teach our children to acknowledge the Trinity, to make acts of love, and to ask for the grace to love more, long before they are in school—and grace will accomplish marvels within them. It is as simple as finding a child alone with you, kneeling with him to say, "Let's think of the Father, the Son and the Holy Ghost in our souls, and tell them we love them, and ask them to help us love them more." This God cannot resist.

Again, love was the reason why Mary's will could so perfectly embrace God's will. One increases in love, one understands better how vast is His love, and His will begins to appear a manifestation of His love.

It was God's will for Mary that she bear Christ—that she bear Him in a stable, and care for Him, that she nurse Him and wash Him and clothe Him, that she care for Him in Bethlehem and Egypt and Nazareth, weaving, cooking, washing, cleaning, teaching; and she be His servant, His mother, His confidante, His comfort. And it is when we hear Christ say, "Whatsoever you do to these, the least of My brethren, you do unto Me," that we understand wherein, after the love of God, our imitation and our children's imitation of Mary must lie. We must see Him in all men, and seeing Him, we must serve Him. Mary's way is the way.

With Mary to Serve Christ

This is why the imitation of the love; first, to see the Christ in men. This is why the imitation of the virtues: to serve Christ in men. A child's imitation of Mary has nothing to do with superficialities and attitudinizing. It has to do with how one lives, and with whom one lives, from every morning to every night of every day of every year. Because the mother and the father, the brother and the sister, the baby, the neighbor, the bus driver, the school teacher—all of them are other Christs.

Gently, patiently, beginning when they are ever so young, a mother and a father explain this mystery of the Christ to be seen in each other. The most perfect, the most lucid exposition of it is, again, His "Whatsoever you do to these..." He said it again, another way, when He threw Saul from his horse and cried: "Saul, Saul, why dost thou persecute Me?" So there is Christ in Peter, and in Jamie, and in John, and Christ in Monica and Christ in Stephen. And Monica, who is eight, and is called to care for Stephen, to change his diapers and mop his chin, to dry his tears and butter his bread— Monica is taught that she changes, and mops, and dries, and butters for Jesus, and she does these things obediently and humbly and tenderly and with love—as Mary. Monica, when she has to change a very soiled diaper (her mother in bed sick) will have to turn away to keep from retching, then asks the Blessed Mother (who knows all about diapers) to help her, give her the grace to do it—and then she will get it done.

Training Children to Be Brave

For Mary does answer their prayers and give them the courage they need. We had quite an experience recently, anticipating shots for measles. The little boys facing the ordeal had twenty-four hours to repair to the Blessed Virgin and ask for the grace to keep their mouths shut and not to howl anymore at the prospect of visiting the doctor. May that most pure Lady be eternally praised—she took them in hand, listened to their problem, and evidently talked turkey to them. We never had such heroism before! Everytime anyone weakened there was a shout to Mary; we actually had smiles all the way to the doctor's and only yells for about thirty seconds.

I wish all mothers would try this; for I am sure it was a genuine spiritual experience. John Michael (who is four) is especially terrified of pain; for him particularly relationship with Mary must be made to be what it should be: quite virile, not sticky with mush and goo.

The Joy of Mary

Mary is perfect for children. She herself was a girl, raised Christ (a real boy), was far and away the most enchanting child God ever made (with the exception of course of Jesus), and was never a bore, never a prissy mouth smooth-your-skirts kind of child, and was all they find glamorous in a woman. Beautiful—ohhhh! adventures? bushels! brave? the bravest! She knew a million stories to tell. She told Little Boy Jesus all about God (their favorite topic—really...) and on the score of her telling Jesus, can't you imagine the conversation when she taught God about God?

PURITY AND THE YOUNG CHILD

MARY REED NEWLAND

A long, long time ago it seems, I spent a lot of time poring over various techniques offered in print for approaching the subject of the sex education of my children, and filed them all carefully away to await the coming of say, our first child's tenth, perhaps twelfth, year.

Now that the same child is six and in the first grade at school, off shortly after seven every morning to spend her day in the company of a host of unknowns until three in the afternoon, I find suddenly that the bogey "sex education for children" has raised its ugly head a full four or five years ahead of time—and the problem is here, to be solved now and not a year, not even a month from now.

Anyone who has children, or a child, will observe, if he is honest and observant, that before they are even a few short years along in this life they discover and are inclined to explore their own bodies. As soon as they are able to talk, all this is accompanied by innocent comments and questions

about their various parts, and to assign more than just innocent curiosity to these performances is being unsavory and
suspicious. However, knowing full well that, contrary to the
sentimentalists, to the pure all things are not forever pure, it
is foolish to let this first opening of a subject that concerns
the very life of a soul, eventually, be brushed aside as something that will probably die a natural death and is better
ignored than given undue attention. Undue attention can be
as disastrous as no attention at all, and it is not undue attention, but just attention, that is called for. With the first opening of the door, the first faint light of sex consciousness that
dawns in a child's mind, also comes the opportunity for in-
augurating a relationship with the child which, if handled
wisely, will increase in breadth and depth and capacity until
that fatal stage is reached where sex, with all its contingent
danger, is a problem that moves in to stay until adolescence,
the teens and finally a fully ripened maturity have been met
and conquered.

One wonders why in this particular phase of growing up
the ties between the parent and the child take the maximum
strain and end so many times with no means of communication left at all in regard to the subject. Why do mothers and
fathers suddenly awaken to find their children are discussing
sex at length with their friends' mothers, but avoiding it with
their own? And when questioned, why do so many young
people answer, "But I just can't talk to my mother, my father, about sex. I don't know exactly why—somehow it's em-
barrassing. I don't think they'd really understand." Which
isn't what they mean at all, though they may not know it.
Obviously any two people who have known a union intimate enough to produce children "understand" about sex. It
isn't lack of understanding that is the answer. It is the three-
way relationship that is missing—the relation of *child to par-*

ent to sex. And as exaggerated as it may sound at first, maybe the answer to this whole thing lies in that first gentle opening of the door at the age of two or three or four years, when hardly more than babes they discover and begin to ask questions about their bodies.

There's nothing nasty about the human body. Human minds are capable of high nastiness, but the body itself is good and beautiful and purposeful, and incidentally, marvelously well-designed. After all, God invented, if one may use the word here, human bodies and as yet few of us have been capable of suggesting any very intelligent improvements. What transpires in our relation of mind to body is apt to result in a thoroughly nasty mess—but in the beginning, after Baptism, the relationship is rich with promise: soul, enclosed in a marvelously useful body, governed by a mind which in turn is fed on the grace distributed to the soul. But that's not all, is it? There is hidden within the combination of the three another even as marvelous attribute, elusive and provoking, and that is free will. And it is the will darting about like a wild ungoverned thing that can throw the monkey wrench into the whole—that can wrench the relationship of the other three, and distort and destroy and cause havoc until the body and the mind and the soul are at war with each other, and the end God had in view when He combined the three is thwarted and finally, tragically, rejected.

So, with the child in his baptismal innocence we do not have to question the perfection of soul, nor the existence of the good and useful body, nor the possibilities for perfection that lie before the as yet untaught mind. But as the psychologists are so fond of pointing out to us, the child, untaught and untamed, is a healthy little animal (albeit, an animal with a soul) and left to his own resorts will undoubtedly proceed in short order to his own destruction. This, so far, is all very well and we agree with the psychologists. However, we begin to part company with the majority of them when we contemplate what direction we wish the teaching and taming of the child to take. The psychologists, like the rest of the moderns in our world, are bent on training these little animals so they will be adjusted, well-behaved, self-fulfilled members of the society of our day. While we would have them be members of the Communion of Saints—capable of adjusting to the society of any day, not because of any exposure to education or psychologically sound guidance, but because they have securely in their minds their *raison d'être*: to know God and love Him and serve Him on this earth and give glory to Him forever in Heaven.

All things are in relation to this; there is nothing that is not. And when we are faced with the dilemma that is what and how to dive in and get on with sex information to children, it helps a lot to clear the decks of all other considerations. All things that God created are good, good and beautiful, and the unfolding of the mysteries of the body can be as wholesomely exciting as some are capable of making them unwholesomely exciting.

Early Explorations

Let us start with the littlest child and his first question. Usually it has to do with his eliminative system. His first reactions to these functions are pleasant ones, the result is comforting because the body's comfort depends on the well-ordered functioning of these various parts. But then little ones discover that in addition to the basic function of these interesting parts, there is also a certain pleasant sensation attached to exploring them. This infantile exploration can usually be outwitted by seeing that small children are securely pantied and given other distractions to absorb their attention. But there is something of which we must beware. Children who are meditative, who, when hurt or puzzled or sent off alone to their rooms as punishment, do not so often strike out or rebel or challenge as creep away and nurse their injuries—children of this type are quite capable of seeking solace in a *totally unconscious* indulgence of these same pleasant sensations. There is hardly a grain, if any at all, of awareness in what they do. There is surely, in the beginning, no ill will, no real guilt involved. There is an overwhelming sense of hurt and abandonment which children are so capable of feeling, and finding no comfort or sympathy anywhere else they seek to comfort themselves. This may make the more squeamish parents squirm and protest: "But my child never did anything like *that!*" No! Are you so sure? What you are so repelled by is something as old as the ages, and children have done it down the ages and good ones, too, innocent ones who were pure of heart and unaware they were doing it. And characteristically, it is the parents whose children, they assure us, never did that—whose very blindness and refusal to entertain the possibility turns them into suspicious, scolding, nagging accusers and snoopers if they happen on the occasion. And with first meeting in fact, their very attitude slams shut a door that might well have led to a mutually enriching confidence between both parent and child.

You may like to fool yourself that this first awareness and acquaintance of the infant, the little pre-schooler, with his own body and its pleasant sensations is not *really* related to the business of sex education for children, but it is the root of it, the beginning and the first flowering, and if you don't start with it here, you'll find you've opened a book in the middle some day and wonder why it doesn't make sense when you've never known the beginning.

How exactly would one handle such a revelation, though?

Children, until they have cause to cease, are very frank and open with their opinions. Once they have learned that certain opinions or attitudes, when voiced, produce certain unhappy results, they are capable of practicing very successful deceits, erecting very convincing camouflages. So it is practically guaranteed that if a mother or father would approach the small child whom they have observed interested in this particular exploration with a calm, pleasantly inquiring manner, the child will be equally calm and pleasant about discussing it. Until he has been told certain things are wrong, there is no reason for suspecting they are. In fact, he wastes very little time in his early years weighing whether things are wrong or right. It is his association of cause and effect, wrong and punishment, which eventually organizes the machinery for determining what is wrong and what is right. Suppose a mother does then inquire pleasantly and discover that her child has made a rather intimate acquaintance with certain parts of his body. She needn't be surprised or shocked—he isn't the first child to do so, nor will he be the last, nor should it be so totally unexpected. As we have said, they come perfect in many ways but untaught and untamed. Well, she may explain, it really isn't quite the thing to do. She understands, of course, that it can be quite pleasant—but that is not the purpose for which God created this part of the body, and as God has a special reason for creating it, He wishes us to use it for that purpose only. Now this is one of the first times, she may go on, when something that feels pleasant and seems to be all right, isn't. And this is what she has meant when she has told the child on occasions before that it is sometimes not so easy to be good. In fact, it is often hard, but the harder it is, the more pleased God is when one succeeds in being good.

Then instead of leaving it all purely theoretical, the

mother can proceed to a practical attack. When the child thinks maybe it would be pleasant to indulge this particular fancy, he must remember: "No, God doesn't want me to do this." Then he can try a little trick on himself and see if it doesn't work. Fold his hands tightly together and quickly say to the Blessed Mother: "Please, Blessed Mother, help me to be pure."

Now just try that next time, his mother may say, and see if it doesn't make a big difference. That is what pure means—it has many meanings, but for little children most of all it means remembering how good God made their bodies, and how useful He made them, and that they must use them only for the purposes for which God made them. That is what the child means when he prays every morning: "Please help me to be pure and good and keep me safe from harm."

After this, it is possible to make a kind of secret conspiracy out of the business, with the child and the mother and the Blessed Mother the sole conspirators. At night in the security of their goodnight hug, the mother can whisper, "Don't forget—ask Blessed Mother to help you to be pure—just see if she doesn't." And you may believe this or not as you wish, but a child will take such an interest in this miniature warfare that he or she will come periodically and from the depths of a bear hug, whisper at any odd hour of a day, "I'm trying very hard to be pure." I have been the receiver of such a secret revelation.

For parents who have honestly never met with this problem, an undue amount of space may seem to be allotted to it. And too, they may be inclined to herd all such children into a category that includes inferiors of a variety of types, both intellectual and moral. Let's air that notion out right now. That this early acquaintance with bodily sensations can be innocent is unquestioned and the fact that most books on child care cover the problem in some detail seems to prove that it is a fairly common thing. What is important is this: that it not be confused with the more serious transgression of the same nature which older children, boys particularly, are apt to indulge in later years. This is not the same thing at all. This is innocent and the result of simple, accidental exploration on the part of normally curious children. However—there lurks in the shadows those years that are soon to be upon children when it can become a problem of major dimensions, and to say there is no connection, that the one is not capable of developing into the other, is sticking one's head in the sand. There isn't a parent alive who wouldn't shudder to entertain even the merest hint of such performances on the part of his adolescent children. And yet trying to meet serious sin, at the eleventh hour and after there has been some experience with it, experimental or otherwise, is a very tough proposition. Adolescents and teenagers are not inclined to be carried away by a last-minute introduction to the subject of purity. Perhaps several generations ago, the overall attitude of the world in general toward public discussions of sex made a big difference in the way children received their sex enlightenment. But today's father and mother, trying to instill principles of Christian purity in their children, find themselves backed against the wall and faced with a counter-propaganda via the movies, suggestive magazines, conspicuously promiscuous moderns which, but for the grace of God, they are at a loss to fight. The only rule of thumb that exists today in regard to impure performances on the part of the young and old alike seems to be—"don't get caught." Purity consciousness is at as low an ebb as it has ever been since the beginning of the race—and in most cases the very word carries one connotation only, that having to do with a nationally advertised brand of soap which is ninety-nine and forty-four one hundredths percent pure.

The time to start establishing the norm is as soon as the child is capable of applying the word *purity* to some part of his own experiences, even the innocent ones, that the concept can be formed..."this is purity, dear, knowing how good your body is, how wonderfully God formed it, and being very careful not to abuse it in any way."

He Is Not Alone

And then there is this, too, which is as important a part of the strategy as connecting the word with one's own personal behavior: the child need not struggle with his little temptations alone. God wants him to be pure, granted, but there is one whose very synonym is Purity and she is the Mediatrix of all Graces, including those to help guard and cultivate the virtue. Mary, whose experience with the Holy Childhood makes her the first protector of children, Mary, whose wisdom so vastly outspans prudishness, is eager, willing, in truth has begged over and over in her apparitions and her references to the horrible impurity in the world today, to be made the mediatrix in our personal lives as we struggle for strength in this battle. Arm the child with a knowledge of what purity means in relation to his own body, and arm him with the company of the Queen of Angels. Open the door and give him the security of knowing she is there, eager to help, and impress him over and over with the conviction that she is watching, hoping he will win, and always so pleased, so delighted when he does. There cannot be too much stress laid on the revelation that God and Mary are watching, always—but be sure to accompany it with the assurance that they watch lovingly, hopefully and eager to help. And if there is failure, let the picture be one of a saddened and disappointed Heavenly Father and Mother—not a wrath-

ful pair who will draw in their skirts and wash their hands of
the culprit. Teach them an ejaculation, like the above, "Please,
Blessed Mother, help me to be pure," and repeat and repeat
and repeat, until the refrain is part of their unspoken meditations, their store of associations with the very word purity.
And contemplate the sum total of grace, which is always
given for the asking, which will pour into the soul addressing such a supplication to the Giver of Graces. Then when
the serious temptations are met, when there steals at last into
the consciousness what all these years of preparation were
aimed at, there has been already established the habit of crying for help in the first throes of trial. To plead and beg and
exhort the youngster involved in the toils of a first love affair
to call on the Blessed Mother for protection is good—but
how overwhelmingly the passions can succeed in drowning
out even the most sincere exhortation, even the most sincere
intention.

That part of the Church's training for her young, in catechism and doctrine classes and within the four walls of the
parochial classroom, includes this stress on purity is true.
But just how much effective substituting can our priests do
for the parents in the brief hours of instruction time? This is
a matter that calls for twenty-four-hour-a-day consciousness,
and it must grow out of a home where no subject is taboo,
where no questions are ignored, but where no aberrations go
unnoticed. It must grow in an atmosphere that is above prudishness, that is the essence of modesty without disintegrat-
ing into mere daily preaching, and unless parents are willing
to take stock of their very young with all their curiosities,
with their potentials for both good and evil, and relate them
all to the whole, which is life in Christ, there is going to be a
lot of precious time lost and a lot of last minute sprinting to
catch up when it is almost too late.

As I had thought that sex education would probably not be a problem met for a good ten or twelve years, so I included with that filed-away material the business of explaining how babies come into the world. However, the other day my three oldest children, six, five and three, were informed by a five year old neighbor that their mommy was going to have a baby. They accepted this piece of information without noticeable effect, having been already informed that God was sending us another baby sometime this summer. Frankly, they have come to sense there is a cycle of some twelve or sixteen months or so, at the end of which a new baby always puts in an appearance. So the announcement coming from both their parents as well as the neighbor child was something they welcomed but took in their stride as part of the normal course of events in our family. Failing to get the desired reaction from them, however, the neighbor child went one further and revealed that the information was available to her, not because she had been informed, but because she had taken stock of this mommy's changed anatomical design and drawn the only conclusion possible.

Now here was a piece of news that was really startling! All our children have seen our cat bear kittens. Cats have a way of changing shape before kittens are born, and even the simplest juvenile mind can put two and two together, sooner or later, and get—kittens. They happened on her in the throes of her delivery twice (kitty is shockingly casual in her choice of delivery room) so the process had ceased to be a mystery. Then last summer one of the cows pastured on our land evaded her owner when he came to fetch her home in time for her blessed event, and sought refuge in the woods where we later found her, also in the process of delivering a new life into the world. This they discussed in a thoroughly wholesome manner and came forth with the conclusion, after reflecting on the changed shape of the mother cow over the months previous, that the result accounted for the noted increase in mother cow's proportions.

So the evening of the day of great revelation, after the younger ones were in bed and asleep, I discovered my six-year-old lying awake and gazing meditatively at the cows (all in various stages of anticipating this year's crop of calves) grazing outside her window.

"I guess they're going to have babies, too," she reflected. "They look like they are, don't they?"

I agreed and waited for the next comment.

"Is it the same with mommies having babies as it is with animals?"

This Is It!

Bang! And sex education for children was a problem of the present moment, between myself and my six-year old child. And it would never do to let her hang in mid-air, associating what she knew of the cat and her kittens, the cow and her calf, with this longed for, prayed for, blessed baby we'd soon be introducing to her. There was no choice but to dive in.

No, it wasn't quite the same. God made animals strong and hardy, and they had their babies wherever they were best suited to have them, sometimes in the fields, sometimes in a barn or even, as with kitty, in the kitchen woodbox. But with mommies it was different. They had to have their babies in the hospitals, or in their houses up in their rooms. And with mommies there had always to be someone to help, like the good doctor we love so much, or nurses or members of the family, like aunts or sisters.

But that wasn't exactly what she meant, she said. She meant—did the baby come the same way the baby kittens and the baby calf came? N. said that mothers had babies inside of them before they were born. Well, did they come the same way animal babies did?

I might say I groaned inwardly, but there wasn't time for that. One's mind darts frantically, clutching for the right words, and there is the overwhelming sense of the importance of the relationship the answers to these questions is going to establish between the two of you. No time for concocting, and certainly no time for lying. There is only one way open, to tell the truth, with God's help, as gently and as discreetly and as wholesomely as you can.

So we plunged on. In a way babies come the same way. God has made a special place in all mothers through which, when it is time, babies come into the world.

Without waiting for any further embroidery she bluntly asked, "Where?"

As carefully as I could I explained where. And made it very clear that since all things God does are good, there could be no question but His way of having babies come into the world was the best of all possible ways and therefore good and pure and holy. And once again we were back to purity, and why one is careful (particularly careful with this new understanding of the body and its apertures) not to abuse one's body. Now she could understand, couldn't she, why we must think of our bodies as holy and good, and must carry ourselves about with a special sense of caring for a piece of God's handiwork. And when we remembered that not only did the body have all these good and noble uses, but also that the Father, the Son and the Holy Ghost lived within the soul, which was itself within the body, as long as we are good—then it made all the difference in the world how we felt about ourselves, our bodies, and all the parts of our bodies.

There flashed through my mind what Eric Gill had written about his own bewilderment when confronted with all these puzzles as a boy, particularly his first struggle with temptation. His first information about his little boy parts ("Shame on you!") had come to him tainted with the sense of "unclean." Later, when the question of sex raised its head, he was told these same parts were "sacred." And within the young mind, a war began trying to justify the two conflicting notions—how could one's parts be both unclean and sacred at the same time? And he dismissed the ideas his elders were trying to impress upon him as being no more or less than part of a great confusion from which they suffered as well as he, and he made up his mind for himself. This part of his autobiography caused much discussion and consternation at the time, but if nothing else it certainly underlined the terrible need for an understanding on the part of parents of the tremendous interest this whole subject holds for children—and young children, too.

Take It Easy

At such an early age, six or so, the question is apt to be asked, how did the baby get there? But to be told that God has planted a seed within the mother is sufficient to quiet any further curiosity and of course going further than this with such young children would be unthinkable, and, to my mind, a crime of major proportions. What one must try to do with these very young and their questions is be honest, instill a sense of respect, and establish a camaraderie between the parent and child in respect to the subject. The father and the mother both (and this must not always be just "woman talk," it is terribly important that fathers take over their share of the dispensing of this new wisdom, either alone or together with the mother and the children) must tackle the problem with the kind of attitude that promises unending patience in the answering of questions and at no time distaste or disinclination to answer or discuss or help. Keeping this door open is, next to instilling the knowledge of God and His love within them, about the most important thing of all in the life of the child.

There have been children at school and in the immediate vicinity who have evidenced an appetite for unsavory discussions about all these things, and the innocent reports of conversations attempted with my own bairn have several times proved very alarming, to say the least. So far they are perfectly frank to report these sallies on the part of other children. And so far, thank God, they have felt no need to get involved. We have a standard reply to give children who want to whisper and giggle about such things, and that is: "I can talk about that as much as I want to with my mother— and it isn't very nice to talk about it with anyone else." And so they do. They go through stages, each one of them, where their bodies are tremendously absorbing topics of conversation, and we have had some long, may I say "calf" sessions?— on the subject. And it seems to exhaust the store of questions, and satisfy the curiosity, and the ideas are laid to rest for another little while. But one does not fool one's self that there are times when vigilance is no longer needed. What with the world shouting sex from all sides, it is to be expected that normal, observant children are going to be reminded—no matter how pure their minds are—periodically, and find their interest once again aroused.

There is another wonderful part of God's plan which seems to escape a lot of people when they get discussing sex education for children, and that is the natural, orderly process by which He sees fit to educate them Himself through the increase and multiplication of the Christian family. The

husband and wife who enter their marriage with enough
faith in God to feel He can be trusted to design—plan—
their family for them will find His wisdom in the matter of
sex and children is boundless. For instance, the prime purpose for which He designed the feminine bosom has been all
but drowned in propaganda for the display of same as part of
baiting and catching the male. I remember when I was expecting my first child asking my doctor if I might nurse my
baby. Among all my friends who were new mothers, there
was not one who made even an attempt to, and somehow in
my stupidity I had concluded that the modern age had made
it a thing of the past—well-nigh impossible for the young
modern. Doctor D. snorted and said, "God didn't make you
the way He did just to be decorative! Of course you can
nurse your baby—at least you can try."

Then, too, in the large family where there are older children who must help with the care and training of the younger
ones, it is all part of the day's routine to help the little ones to
and from the "baffroom" and in and out of the tub. All of
which helps to eliminate any undue interest in brotherly and
sisterly anatomy. Nor does this necessarily rule out the formation of a distinct sense of modesty in the young. During
the early years when children need help with their baths,
etc., there is no sense of either the modest or the immodest
in them. They need help and it is common sense for the
older members of the family to help them, in the process
becoming quite used to the way God put them together and
eventually failing even to be aware of the differences in their
arrangements. Later when they are capable of caring for themselves, it is quite natural to explain, and expect, that one
likes to be alone to dress and bathe—and privacy in this
respect is the order of the day.

Each of the various activities involving the body and its

purpose is, in greater or lesser degree, like individual tesserae in the whole of a mosaic. Each has an important relationship to the establishment of a sense of purity in the young mind, and the paradox seems to be that establishing the sense of purity depends on a wholesome acknowledgement of all God has put together to create the human body, *not in prudishly avoiding it.*

It is all good and for a purpose, and learning about it the right way can be an inspiring way of giving glory to God. What a wonderful world it would be if the sense of goodness and purposefulness of the body were suddenly to fall into place in every man's mind. That's a large order—but if all fathers and mothers would dedicate themselves to revealing these very things to their own children, we'd be off to a good start.

CHILDREN AND THE VALUE OF MONEY

MARION MITCHELL STANCIOFF

One of Charles Adams' sunnier cartoons depicts a mother showing a friend a basement gameroom where two small children are busy over a little still, and saying, "We don't believe in allowances, they have to earn every cent themselves..."

The parents who believe in allowances explain that a regular allowance teaches a child to plan. They assure their child a definite weekly or monthly sum and it is earnestly agreed between them that the child will supply certain of his wants—say his lunch at school—from that sum and will not ask for more. The child thus learns the prices of those things he is interested in—which he has probably been aware of since he was able to read figures—and can calculate how much he can spend on ice cream cones, comics, movies, and the other delights of youth. He gets into the habit of regular amusements and it is piously hoped these regular habits will be carried on into later life.

The parents who believe in earning every cent explain that only earning money will teach a child to be independent. They steadfastly resist their child's pleas for money and dutifully rejoice when the latter brings home his first dime. The child may spend his school time cogitating schemes for turning a more or less honest penny and his after-school time putting the schemes into practice, but the main thing is that silver has crossed his palm and he is henceforth a fledgling member of the great plutocracy and can be relied on to rely on himself through life.

The Value of Money

The holders of both these theories add that *it teaches a child the value of money.* Now if there is one thing that is quite obvious in our civilization, it is the value of money. Not only does money talk, but it cries out loud from every billboard, every scrap of newsprint, every shop window, every entertainment, and many sermons. It makes such a noise that it shuts out most other sounds. It is the business of parents to awaken their children's attention to less strident calls and to teach them first the values which are less immediately apparent than those of money.

Any fool—and all the more any child with his wits about him—knows that money is a good thing. It is delightful to have, full of increase for oneself. This is so pleasing to natural laziness and greed that it is surprising men had been civilized so long before they thought of money. Its invention is usually credited to that nation of fabulous business men, the Lydians. Until they popularized the use of coins as tokens of wealth (probably in the sixth century before Christ) people got what they wanted by barter. Barter can be cumbersome and the use of currency improved the tempo of trade. It also improved the chances of cheating. The modern financial system has made real goods still more remote from the consumer and so lends itself to novel forms of dishonesty ever more elaborate and hard to detect.

Money is less and less connected with goods. It can change hands a number of times and grow or shrink quite wonderfully without goods entering the scene at all. It is therefore essential to distinguish between money and property.

Money Is Never More Than a Convenience, While Property Is Always a Necessity

The Church teaches us to respect ownership of even the least material goods because, being partly made of transitory matter, we need matter to sustain ourselves. And being partly made of imperishable spirit, we must by an orderly use and conservation of material goods, deliver ourselves from continual preoccupation with them in order to free ourselves to attend to our spiritual needs. Although property is a necessary safeguard of bodily life, it can, as Jesus warned, be a danger to spiritual life. Some wise people for that reason delegate the holding of property to others.

Nevertheless, even the poorest beggar or a saint like Benedict Joseph Labre is not totally without property; he owns his rags or his rosary. And rearing a family requires more than that, especially in a cold climate. The papal utterances particularly insist on a modicum of property—the ownership of some goods—as a necessary safeguard for the liberty of the spirit. If the popes of modern times have particularly defended the principle of property it is because that principle has been particularly attacked. In the past the egotistic use of property had been attacked, and the excessive acquisition of property had been attacked, but until Proudhon exclaimed "Property is theft," the natural right to own things had never been seriously questioned.

The no-right-to-property heresy has made such strides in a century that a great part of the world's inhabitants profess it—some by conviction, and more under duress. The seed of this heresy has spread so fast because the ground was plowed for it by another heresy: *the cult of money.* To see the truth of this exemplified, we need only look at the very numerous cases of young communists who were raised in well-to-do or even very wealthy homes. Usually it turns out that the parents' excessive preoccupation with money initially disgusted the youngster and started the reaction against all property holders and the social system which upholds their rights. The Church warns us against both heresies by defending the rights not of money but of property, and defending the rights of poverty as well. Too often materialistic societies which uphold the rights of property deny the rights of poverty. They like to make prosperity the proof of virtue and poverty the badge of worthlessness, and they incline to outlaw what they cannot legislate away.

Property then is a prop, a staff giving us staying power and thus, up to a point, ensuring liberty. It gives a man with a family the power to leave a bad employer, to speak his mind freely, to elect and serve whom he pleases in the knowledge that his children will not starve. A man with the essentials of life assured is not dependent on a paycheck. He is his own man and therefore more directly, God's.

The Danger of Money

In educating her children the Church has always upheld the rights of property and emphasized the dangers of money. Until she was more than three quarters of her present age, she forbade the taking of any interest on money. Her greatest theologian held that money can never legitimately breed money. She was careful to induce a feeling of guilt about money lest men love it too much. Thus inculcated with contempt for money-as-an-end, Christians came to despise those who made it their end. The miser and the usurer were not only figures of fun but of loathing. Work to be respectable had to be productive, productive either in creating goods or in serving people. (And in this military service was naturally included, though it may now seem to us often erroneously.) Money-making as a business—that is, brokerage—being anti-social was held in cruel scorn. This was the prevailing attitude throughout Christendom until the breakaway from the Church in the sixteenth century.*

A Way of Bringing Up Children

But many still try in one way at least to maintain the old ideal. They still do what they can to bring their children up free from the thought of money. This does not mean that they leave them free to spend as they like. On the contrary, more often than not they do not let them spend at all. They

---

*The theory that the Protestant Reform was the chief factor in altering the attitude of Christendom toward money was put forward by the non-Catholic scholars Lombart, Weber and Tawney early in this century, and it is now held by a great many objective historians. However, a great economic historian who is also a great Christian, Amintore Fanfani, exploded this theory almost twenty-five years ago. He proved that the attitude of the Papacy toward money had begun to vacillate by the end of the fifteenth century when the popes resorted to patronizing money lenders on a large scale and when the mercantile Republics of Venice and Genoa developed such vast banking operations that by sheer massiveness, usury began to appear respectable. The two misnomers Reform and Renaissance were merely two symptoms of a general fermentation of thought and breakdown of principle in high places of which the origins are not clear to us.

This was still the attitude of the country gentry and of the landed peasantry in Catholic lands down to our own times. In such families right down to the first World War, the only careers considered honorable, apart from agriculture, were the liberal professions or military or administrative service. Trade was still where St. Thomas had put it, lowest among the legitimate occupations, and speculation was on a par with cheating at cards.

The pristine purity of these principles was no longer apparent to a generation impoverished by wars and revolutions. Many a youngster has turned away from what had come to seem mere narrow and musty tradition and sought his fortune in trade or finance.

hold that a child in his father's house has all he needs: shelter, food and clothing, and also entertainment, he has the conversation of the family, of servants, and of friends to listen to, the wide world of nature to look at, books to read, skills to learn, jobs to help with, and games to play. Children are encouraged to make music or to draw or write and act, or otherwise provide their own enjoyment. Purchased pleasures are not even thought of except perhaps as an extraordinary birthday treat. Children raised in this way know that *money must not be thrown away* because those around them do not spend it carelessly. They know that money may be given away because they see it used to relieve some of the ills around them. They live in perfect freedom and in complete dependence as do the birds of the air which take no thought for the morrow for their father provides what they need. The less he has, the less they get. They share in the family troubles as well as in its joys. In moments of financial difficulty they are proud to help the family group by making do with as few things as they can, and do not feel frustrated like the child who has been trained to expect a definite sum on the first of every month. In times of financial prosperity, children brought up in this old way are not given more than they need, but are taught the joy of being able to give more away.

On holidays and birthdays and such great occasions, a child may receive gifts of money which vary and are as indeterminate as the sunshine and the rain that come from heaven. This money a wise parent teaches a child to save in order to spend it generously when occasion arises. It may be for presents for others, it may be for useful or lovely things for himself which his parents do not provide him with; it may be, and should often be, to help people in need.

Thus the child is less likely to become a fritterer than the

child who is given money every day. He is less likely to become an addict of bought pleasures than the child who receives a regular allowance. And he is less likely to grow calculating than those who have to earn each penny that they use. The child's mind is free and so is his heart, and such freedom from the thought of money, from the thoughts even of everyday necessity, is the highest luxury, the noblest liberty of man.

Calculation Is the Enemy of Wonder

There is no doubt that calculation is the enemy of wonder. For we cannot objectively admire what we are trying to acquire, nor honestly revere what we itch to exploit. Wonder—which is simply disinterested admiration and examination—is said to be the beginning of philosophy (no doubt because humility is its essential condition) and true love of wisdom is, we know, the pathway to heaven. To encourage calculation in a child is to curtail his capacity for wonder and to cut him off from his natural heritage of joy in this world and the next. The child brought up to develop his mind and heart and senses is incalculably richer than the child trained to develop his business sense. He will want little and need less but give generously and be able to enjoy immensely.

The child taught to expect a regular sum at a certain time is being unconditioned for life when all is irregular and uncertain. He is being given the impression that his portion must come to him, that he somehow has a right to it, that his parents, or his employer or the world, owes him a living, and if it fails him there is a good chance he may get disgruntled, discouraged and depressed.

Money—The Criterion of Value?

Still less prepared for life is the child who is sent out to earn every penny (unless it be to help his family in need). He begins by doing little jobs for the neighbors and getting paid for them, and unless he is very well brought up, he will soon want to be paid for those he does at home and will not want to do them unless he is paid. He will end up by bargaining with his mother over the price of his help and prefer to sell his services outside where he can demand payment and will be seen less and less at home.

Once a money value is placed on services rendered, money and not love becomes the criterion of value. It is then too late to recreate in the child's soul a true conception of life as created by God; he will always see it as it is deformed by man, "smeared with trade," as Hopkins put it. If a child is not taught by practice and example that *love* is the supreme value he will not learn it though he hears it in church and reads it in books. If he does not learn to make sacrifices of time and effort cheerfully when he is young, he may never learn to make them, but will probably go on accepting his parents' sacrifices until he becomes irked by their weight, then he will leave home to escape from the guilt of doing nothing in return.

Whether a child expects to receive money or is expected to earn money or is just given money whenever he asks for it, the preparation for life is equally inadequate. Parents who give their children money or things whenever they ask for them, parents who do not know how to say "No" (there is a great deal in *how* "No" is said) and parents who start by saying "No" and then give in when the child begins to cry, all do so because it makes life easier. It is of course much easier to give money than to explain why it should not be given, harder to say "No" than "Yes" when other parents always say "Yes." And harder to go on saying "No" even when the child wails and sobs than to give him what he wants. But any parent who is not a fool knows that in the long run this line of conduct only makes life harder both for him and for his child and unless he is a criminal, he will try to stand fast. For he knows that to develop the pleasure-buying habit in a child is to make him a slave of things, potentially a slave of other people and certainly a slave of his own whims.

By beginning too late to say "No" parents teach their children new wants instead of teaching them to be free of wants. They teach them to acquire instead of making, to use and devour instead of producing. They often talk about making their children creative but with such instruction they can only become destructive.

Victims of Parental Indulgence

Instead of protecting them from need, parents fling them into a welter of needs and so deliver them over to greed.

People are surprised that so many young delinquents come
from "nice," wealthy homes. Their surprise is surprising. For
even though in many such homes the earn-every-penny-sys-
tem is used—with the idea that this artificial substitute for
the "hard way" may keep the child straight—it is clear that
children trained from infancy to satisfy all their inclinations
by the use of money will develop more and fiercer inclinations as they grow. He who has never learned to refuse himself anything when he was small will see no reason for refusing himself anything when he is big.

Not only that, but such children soon cease to enjoy the
pleasures of which their parents dared not deprive them. *Too
often money buys not pleasure itself but its symbols only.* The
victims of parental indulgence no longer eat this or buy that
or go to such a place because they like it, they do it because
their crowd says it's fun. They are so anxious to get a kick
out of life that all they get is a kick in the teeth; then follows
frustration, depression and alcoholism or psychoanalysis.

Or else money-bought pleasures become merely alge-
braic symbols for success or prosperity or love. It is a pov-
erty-stricken tongue which spells out love in terms of cor-
sages and motor cars, but many girls are experts at translating this A.B.C. and in equating night clubs and solitaires
with love and marriage. When they get to this point they are
not quite human beings anymore. They can no longer see
the difference between happiness and dulness; money-dazzle
has blotted the distinction out and turned these children of
God into bored and miserable bores.

Changing the System

"Where thy treasure is there is thy heart also." This is a
statement of fact which parents should often repeat to themselves. It will help them to understand how to handle their

children's relation to money. They will need all the help they can get, for it is a delicate and a difficult problem. Today the pressure of society is against Christian family behavior and great tact is required to prevent the child from feeling that he is a lonely victim of parental eccentricity. The only possibility of achieving any step in the direction indicated is to enlist the child actively in the movement of reform by making him aware of other-worldly values before he gets swept up by those of this world.

It is in any case impossible to change the system once a plan has been adopted for the child (or even for a family of children where they are close enough in age to expect more or less similar treatment.) Cutting off an allowance or forbidding a budding commerce or refusing accustomed indulgences would seem arbitrary and unjust and would madden any healthy child. It will only be possible to realize a change in the child's money pattern by a change in the outlook of both parents and children. It can be begun by young parents; it can be more easily carried out if several parents who live in the same neighborhood agree to the same idea. It can be done if schools (and I am thinking particularly of Catholic schools) more vigorously discourage the use of money on their premises and especially the display of money-snobbism among their students. There is a great deal that can and must be done if we are to be freed from slavery to Mammon.

But whatever is done must be done without rigidity or plans that are cut and dried. Every child is infinitely different from every other child and a good father will find means that are individual and fresh in preparing each one of them for life. They should be fresh and individual as are the means used by the Father of us all in preparing each one of us, His children, for life in a world in which there will be neither paying nor giving in exchange—for there will be neither currency nor goods save love and of that we shall have plenty in heaven, if that was where our treasure was on earth.

THE LEAGUE
OF ST. LINIMENT

ED WILLOCK

I am one of that class of people to whom Abraham Lincoln was referring when he said, "You can fool some of the people some of the time." Modest though I am, I refuse membership among his second group of citizens, "You can fool some of the people all of the time." There is a limit to my gullibility. You can't fool me all of the time. After an incredible length of time, I catch on. It is because of this slow but eventual perception that I have finally concluded that there is more to the business of sports than meets the eye.

The occasion of my first awakening was about eleven years ago. I had been trying in an enthusiastic but bungling fashion to stir up my friends to some kind of Catholic social action. We were all recently out of school and currently out of work. It had occurred to me that we might put our heads together and try to make sense out of our common misfortune, although, I admit, I was a bit vague about what we could do about it.

My attack on the lads' inertia was as effective as a bow and arrow assault on an aircraft carrier. In a hyphenated word, I received the "brush-off." Just about the time that I had become accustomed to the social standing of a pariah, a new prospect loomed on the horizon. He was a school friend who had entered the seminary but was recalled by an aging mother who needed his support. "Ah!" I thought, "here is a welcoming ear. A young fellow who had aspired to the priesthood should be just the boy to interest in Catholic social action!" My hopes were short-lived. The ex-seminarian immediately found a new outlet for the zeal he could no longer turn to the priesthood. It wasn't the lay apostolate. It was the league of St. Liniment. He became a sports fanatic.

For three months I waged a losing campaign. I suggested a study club...he went to the "Y" to play handball. I thought we might read the papal encyclicals...we read the sports page. I hoped we might stir up some new converts...we stirred up new team-mates. When the three months were up, I had developed an excellent backhand, I knew the batting average of every man in both Leagues, I had a bleacher tan, I was hoarse from shouting above the strident voice of the sports announcer...but I had lost a lay apostle.

Since that time I have become aware of the new brand of Catholic action: the League of St. Liniment. I have attended many meetings, lectures, study clubs, and discussions. The topics covered at such meetings ranged from unionism to the liturgy. These meetings, which are the necessary preliminary to any kind of social action, were almost always predominantly attended by women. The women are militant, zealous, and more than willing do do their share. The boys and men are, with but few exceptions, I find, in the St. Liniment League.

To find out where the men were throwing their weight, one needed only to look at the sports page. The thing read like a litany: St. Athanasius swamps Our Lady of Sorrows... The Friars nose out a victory over the Crusaders...Francis X. O'Hara, coach of St. Athleticus, predicts downfall of Sacred Heart...Father Aloysius McGee feted at Holy Name Society Sports Nite...Sodalists pay tribute to winner of marathon...etc.

It is a noteworthy fact that the American Catholic teen-agers who at the present time are gracing the diamonds and the gridiron are the very age, and class, and sex of Catholics who in Europe constitute the backbone and spearhead of Catholic Action. The JOC in Belgium, the most glorious group of militants the Church has produced, are, in the main, teenage youths.

Supposing, for a moment, that the American Church could dispense with the services of the young fellows and leave them to their games, how about the older men? What becomes of them when the paunch appears, and the breath comes harder? They merely move from the League of St. Liniment, Jr. to the League of St. Liniment, Sr. They are the perennial spectators. From early spring to late fall their minds and hearts, news pages, and radio dials, turn to the baseball meccas of America. Between times they placate their appetite for sports with football, basketball, bowling, hockey, golf, tennis and ping-pong.

The amount of attention and daily meditation given during the baseball season to the history being made on the diamond, if turned by the same Catholic men to the history of the Church, would give Christopher Dawson and Hilaire Belloc as wide an audience in the Church as Grantland Rice. The same assiduous attention given to the rules and proce-dures of games and sports, if directed to the moral law and its application by the same Catholics, would remove the necessity of repeated Sunday sermons on elementary catechism. The same determination to master the cryptic lingo of the sports prophets, if turned to mastering liturgical Latin, would show quickly how little the need is for translating the Mass into the vernacular.

Once one becomes aware that the primary enemy of the Church in America is the yawn…indifference, and, once one realizes that indifference indicates that the heart is elsewhere, and, once one realizes where the hearts of most Catholic men lie…then, one wonders whether the enemies' banners, rather than being inscribed with the hammer and sickle, should not be emblazoned with balls and bats.

What's the Score?

The foregoing was written by a man who delights in sports. I enjoy playing a poor game or watching a good one. There is no antagonism between taking delight in music and decrying the practice of fiddling while Rome burns. There is a time and place for all good things. Games are a necessary part of childhood development and they certainly have a place as a form of adult recreation. Within the Christian context a more valid defense of sports can be offered than the usual arguments presented by the current defenders. When the true worth of the game is fully appreciated, it is easier to distinguish between use and abuse.

Games are as integral a part of childhood as work is a part of adult life. In essence, games are make-believe problems stripped of the complexities and seriousness which attend the real problems to which they are analogous. Many talents being developed in the child find an opportunity for obvious development in games. The child can see his own progress in skill, strength, adaptability, and co-operation with his team-mates. With each new effort there is a compensating reward. Failures are punished, but not so seriously as to discourage renewed efforts. The usual steps are from individual effort, alone or in competition with others, to teamwork. In teamwork he comes to realize that his abilities must be co-ordinated with the co-operative scheme or else they are fruitless.

Certain social viruses present among the adult generation have contagiously spread among today's children. One of these is the desire to excel, to beat the other fellow. This competitive spirit is a natural instinct, a fact sufficient to recommend it to today's pagans. The Christian parent, however, recognizes that instinct is hardly the proper basis for human behavior. The spirit of co-operation is eminently more human, and, in the child's games, can be a disposition to supernatural virtue. It disposes the child to charity and justice. He learns

STS. DIAMOND AND GRIDIRON

to subordinate his own desires to the common good, and thus on the gridiron and diamond, he can learn his first lesson in social justice.

Another social virus which has entered the domain of childhood sports comes as a consequence of spectatorism. When I was a kid, we called the disease "grandstanding." In my neighborhood we took great delight in beating the stuffings out of "uniformed" teams. We had a hearty distaste for the team or player who played to the gallery, who played to be admired. I have discovered that now many city fellows won't play baseball or football unless they have uniforms and an audience. By some strange combination of good intentions and bad sense, some parochial groups consider it a work of charity to outfit their children's teams in big league togs. An elementary knowledge of the purpose of the games in relation to childhood development would prove to them that the introduction of spectatorism into games robs them of whatever value they have in developing virtues in the child. The purity of intention, the concentration of enthusiasm on one goal, the total giving—all these wonderful qualities of hard playing, are all weakened by the introduction of the spectator complex. In their place one sees the weakness of today's adults perverting the innocence of childhood: the mixed motive, the half-try, the mediocre ideal, the dramatic pretense and human respect.

When games and sports are thus perverted not only do they fail to build virtue in the boy, they actually soften him up so that he will conform more readily to the similarly false standards common in the adult workaday world.

Mamma's hand is very noticeable in the growing campaign against physical risk in sports. The school footballer now enters the field garbed in an outfit as impregnable as that of an ancient knight. The physical risk has been reduced to about the same level as that of boarding a New York subway train at rush hour. It has been overlooked that physical risk is a normal part of living. Courage in the youth can hardly be quickened when he meets no more fearsome danger than the possibility of a scratched hand. Assurance in the face of travail will not be evoked unless a more formidable problem is posed than that of avoiding a barked shin. Admittedly, in spite of the pads and the precautions, some bones are broken, but not with half as much frequency as those of old ladies who cross busy streets.

Games are for children what work is for men. One must notice how seriously children take their games. Children do not play for fun, they play intently. They are not just killing time. The process of growing up does not change in any way the attitude of the children to those things which occupy their time. The same seriousness, concentration and enthusiasm which children have at their games must be retained as the interest graduates from make-believe problems (games) to real problems (work). Nothing is changed except the object of the youths' attention. In games the situations are serious within their childhood context. When they pass from games to work, their handling of the situations becomes serious within a family or community context. Consequently, two facts emerge: that play is childhood work, and that the attitudes cultivated at play will determine the eventual attitude the child will have to his work.

To permit such perversions of games as hyper-competitiveness or "grandstanding" is not merely to abuse the games, but also to weaken the work qualities of the child.

Professionalism

In professional sports one observes all of the social evils which characterize any field which is commercialized. The

King Midas touch freezes everything into a golden, sterile image of what it had been before his coming. The introduction of the mammon motive into sports causes a completely new orientation of the game. So great is the change that *professionalized*, the game is liable to produce the opposite effect to that educed in its normal state.

Amateur childhood sports contribute greatly to making men out of boys; professional sports contribute greatly to making boys out of men. Those who are at all intimate with professional sportsmen know what a childish lot they are. Their off-hour interests are usually some games other than the ones they are paid to play. Their public demands in them the undisciplined behavior of children. The sports writers call it "color." Even the virtues they manifest are the virtues of a boy rather than a man. The tendency among them is to freeze into a schoolboy pattern, giving a public testimony of eternal adolescence.

A mysticism of innocent and virile virtue has been quietly woven around the sports hero, and it persists despite the obvious fact of a social intimacy between professional sports and the more disreputable areas of society. The breakfast food people juxtapose the sports heroes with smiling ruddy-cheeked boys within the family circle, while the sportsmen themselves, in their choice of off-hour associates (except during the training ritual) frequently are found at home in the vicinity of race tracks, dice, poker chips, gin-mills and night clubs. A sports reporter keeping track of his celebrities would find himself in surroundings that would make a Boy Scout counsellor somewhat embarrassed. He would inadvertently become acquainted with more shady characters, con-men, tipsters, bar-flies and lads who work the angles, than he would ever be able to forget. I am not accusing the sportsmen of vice, but I am not so naive as to further their canonization as espoused on the cornflakes box. My sons will get neither the flakes nor the corn. Neither is very nourishing.

In the Adult Division

Professional sports set the tone in recreation for the American male. As I have pointed out, the professional-spectator brand of sports vary in *kind*, that is, in purpose, intention and motive, from the childhood amateur-participant variety. One form does not evolve from the other. The child-participant is too young to assume a burden of work, so he practices at manhood with the devised situations of games. The adult sport-spectator is a horse of a different color. In most cases he is a man unwilling to assume his share of community burdens, preferring to leave them to the government, his boss, or to chance solution, and turns instead to the imaginary problems of the sports page. As manifested in Catholic circles, this defection accounts for the scarcity of men in the lay apostolate, that new and special obligation prescribed by the Church and made necessary by the times.

It is very easy to understand why men in our times concern themselves so reluctantly with the social order and so fervently with sports. It is not so obvious why such a practice is considered normal, if not virtuous, in some Catholic circles. A man goes to a ball game today to see one of the few kinds of modern enterprises conducted on simple, logical, moral and just principles (I'm referring to the game itself, not the commercial institution). Baseball dramatically poses problems which are resolved in a manner to delight the human heart. To gain victory on the field, the player must work for it. His reputation, chicanery, or knowing the right people cannot be used as substitutes for good pitching, good fielding, or good hitting. The score is proportional to skill and effort. All of these qualities appeal to man's moral sense, and to his elementary justice. In baseball there is a logical sequence of causes and effects. The first man up gets a single...the second man lays down a successful bunt...a long fly from the bat of the third hitter sends the men to second and third...then No. 4 batter gets up, the heavy hitter...what will he do? Will he drive the men home with a base hit? Will the pitcher strike him out? Here is logic to please the simplest soul! Here is drama without sophistry!

What a far cry this make-believe world is from the modern political forum, the sales-room, the stock exchange! In the realm of politics what relation is there now between merit and office? In business who would dare say that reward is in relation to honest effort? the hard worker barely gets along, if *that*. The shrewd calculator, the man who sees the angles, secures the softest feathers and the warmest nest. What logic is there in unemployment? What logic is there in the current housing shortage? We are now audience to the spectacle of our political leaders turning their backs on crises at home and abroad while they load the electoral dice. These processes, political and economic, without logic, without justice, without deference to moral law, drive the citizen to the ball parks for a renewal of his shaken belief in sanity and conscience.

It is to be realized that social and political problems, even under ideal conditions, would present circumstances more complex and more trying than those resolved in sports arenas. As a periodic relief from such cares, games normally will be employed for adult recreation. The fact today, however, is that sports fanaticism is less recreational than escapist. It is less a renewal of energies and perspectives than an escape from the task of resolving the real problems. Spectator sports, the world over, are increasing in popularity in inverse proportion to popular interest in matters of the common good. Games have become substitutes for work.

Who's on First?

Why do sports in parochial circles have an aura of virtue about them? Why, for example, will one find the average curate more willing and capable to direct in matters of sports than in matters of Catholic Action? The fact that one can replace the other in the curriculum of parochial activities should be enough proof that the question of sports is by no means a superficial one. To my mind, this simple matter of priority is a key to the puzzle of Catholic indifference.

Catholicism as manifested by practicing Catholics is best described as being in the stage of retarded adolescence. It is big and muscular: well-attended Masses, busy novena services. It has promise: practicing Catholics in key social positions—mayors, corporation presidents, etc. It has a large appetite: many Communions, Confessions, and other sources of grace. In spite of these things that heighten our expectations, the Faith is not an operative force in society or in family life. At present there is no relation between its potentialities for good and its actual effectiveness.

The same adolescence characterizes the spiritual growth of most Catholics. Our devotion is preparational, a getting ready for sanctity, a some-day-Lord-but-not-yet sort of thing. Then, of course, apostolicity is rare, and this, if not the mark of Christian maturity, is the occasion for it.

The tendency has been to freeze Catholicism at the eighth-grade parochial school level. This stage of development is regarded as the high point and the norm of practical Catholicism. The religious habits of this period in growth are the ones to which the adult feels conscience-bound to return. Sermons, devotional practices, the choice of sticky hymns, are, on the whole, the kind best designed to help an eighth-grader hew to the straight and narrow.

This camp-site was supposedly chosen because all the territory that lies beyond the frontiers of the parochial school is held by the enemy. It is unexplored and unclaimed for Christ. It is the stomping ground for the world, the flesh and the devil, that unholy trinity which has reigned over the secular area for four centuries. The enemy's lines are punctured at one particular spot, and it is a slight bulge indeed. I refer to the area of sports. The Church, in her glory, seldom hits the front pages of our newspapers and never invades the editorial page, but the sports page is another thing! In the realm of sports the Catholic can feel at home. The Irish of Notre Dame have made known the existence of the Catholic Church as a formidable force, if not for producing saints, well, then, quarterbacks. In good conscience, without fear of challenge, the Catholic can invade any arena in America and hold his own. The honor is hollow but nevertheless real.

Because of their consistency with our ideals, sports have been taken to our hearts. This canonization of boy-virtue fits into the all-over pattern of adolescence. Briefly, the scandal is this: we raise the question by our choice of arenas as to whether Catholic virtue can cope with any situation beyond the boyhood stage. "Our boys will do well at the Rose Bowl." *But I wonder what we can do as lay apostles in business, in factories, in politics.* We are actually afraid to set mature Christianity in opposition to mature paganism. We are pessimistic of the results were we to invade the offices and the shops with a dynamic revolutionary Christian spirit, so we satisfy ourselves by challenging the pagans to a ball game.

The choice is quite clear. We can shift the emphasis in male leisure-time activities from sports to the apostolate, or we can go on kidding ourselves that Christian virtue is identical with sportsmanship. The choice is between a mature Christianity worked out or a juvenile Christianity played out. When Catholic Action in the fields of work, of politics, of law, of medicine, of the family, win them the same laurels and the same respect (and, of course, the same kicks in the head) that the activities of Catholics now earn on the gridiron, we will have begun to make an impression. Mature Christians will be facing up to mature problems. When that time comes, what crank could complain about an occasional game of sports?

CRISIS OF FAITH IN YOUTH

ELAINE MALLEY

When we wish to express the serenity, simplicity, and assurance of a faith, we call it childlike. No matter how old a person is, if his faith is like a rock, he is said to have childlike faith. And this is as it should be, because Our Lord Himself said: "Unless ye become like little children, ye shall not enter into the kingdom of heaven."

But St. Paul said: "When I was a child I spoke as a child, I understood as a child, I thought as a child. But when I became a man I put away the things of a child."

If faith is to become a motivating force in the mature adult, these apparent contradictions must be reconciled, and it is during adolescence that they are welded into one truth by living experience. It is during adolescence that the child dies and the adult is born. And yet it is only the survival of the child in the adult that invests his life with all that is receptive to grace.

The Living Tissue

Clearly, what a child's faith is divested of during adolescence is its non-essential element, the seed-coat that protected the living tissue during the formative years. Up to now his faith has rested on borrowed convictions, those of his parents. Up to now his whole world has been encompassed by the reach of their arms. Up to now his parents have stood for him in the place of God.

Now he is beginning to have convictions of his own, he is beginning to find God apart from them, in himself, in his heroes and heroines, in the world about him, and in abstract conceptions of beauty, truth, goodness, justice.

The question that concerns parents is that of the survival of faith in its new habitat. When the children were little one simply told them what to believe and they believed it. They didn't take everything to pieces and examine all its parts under a magnifying glass. They didn't question fundamental doctrines. They didn't have to know the reason for everything.

Violent Extremes

Just as a baby, in learning to stand on his own feet and walk by himself, totters precariously, and occasionally comes a cropper, so the adolescent, in adjusting himself to the new world he is entering, and to the physical, emotional, and intellectual forces that he is encountering for the first time, will fluctuate between violent extremes, assume incongruous poses, and make some pretty spectacular blunders. Most of these reactions are simply temporary stances maintained only until equilibrium can be regained. Under salutary conditions the majority of the wounds suffered at this time are surface bruises.

Indeed they are frequently signs of robust spiritual health.

They represent the skinned knees and scraped shinbones of the pilgrim soul on its first mountain expedition. The adolescent has just discovered a new gift: the flashlight of logic, the ability to link cause and effect, the power to reason things out. And he uses it on everything. He is apt to come out with sweeping statements about things he is discovering for himself. If he is intolerant of the opinions of others, it is because he cannot yet see things under all their aspects, in all their complexities. When he comes across a new idea, it is immediately highlighted by the intense spotlight of his rapt attention. His conclusions are based upon incomplete evidence, but he doesn't know the evidence is incomplete.

It is bad diplomacy to disparage his ideas. This only drives him to defend them more vigorously, and perhaps become more deeply entrenched in them. It is better to listen carefully to what he has to say and point out how logical it is that he should think as he does. Only by trying to see his point of view can the truth be disentangled from error. Once his confidence is enlisted it may be possible to show him other aspects which, because of his inexperience, had not occurred to him.

If his problem is not amenable to reason, because it concerns a matter of revelation that may not be disputed, assure him that what he is grappling with is a mystery, without giving the impression that there is nothing more to be said or done about it. We grow in stature and wisdom by leaning over the abyss of the mysteries of revelation and drinking from its living waters. Quote St. Anselm who said: "I believe in order that I may understand, not I understand in order that I may believe."

Wall of Reserve

The time to suspect that all is not well is when there are

no bitterly contested truths, no stoutly defended heresies, when the adolescent shows an outward spiritless compliance with the formalities of faith, coupled with a stolid indifference to its vital implications, when he tries to hide behind reticence and silence. Of course, a certain amount of reserve and withdrawal is to be expected. The adolescent is discovering that he has a fascinating interior life, and he will guard its privacy jealously against all invasion, except, perhaps, that of a kindred spirit—generally someone of his own age—to whom he may lay bare its treasures. But there is an ominous reticence—no parent who has experienced it can mistake it—which means one of two evils: either a serious infection of the soul by one of the three perennial plagues: the world, the flesh, and the devil; or, what is harder to combat, the contraction of that spiritual paralysis destroying our generation: indifference to matters of religion and of truth.

Ounce of Prevention

Most Christian parents know the measures to take against the first evil—the contagion of sin. An ounce of prevention is worth a pound of cure. Preparation for the crisis of adolescence, for the first serious encounter with temptations against faith and purity, begins in the first years of life, with careful training. The will is trained by the imposition of appropriate duties, by demanding prompt and implicit obedience, and by encouraging voluntary acts of service and self-denial. The understanding is illuminated by Bible stories, by study of the Catechism, by good books and exciting discussions. The personality is enriched by good friends of all ages, creative hobbies, study, the development of wide interests. The soul is fortified by the liturgy, by prayer, and above all, by frequent reception of the sacraments.

Evil Genius

It is the second evil—that of indifference—which parents find it difficult to deal with today. Every generation has its special evil genius which works through the imperfections and failures of society. What makes adolescent faith particularly vulnerable today is not so much spectacular immorality, although the commercial exploitation of vice and sex and sensationalism in movies and periodicals plays its part in undermining our youth. These flagrant scandals have their root in the secularism which permeates the very air we breathe.

For youth secularism frequently wears the garments of idealism. It generates the fallacy that from the stores of our personal experience we can concoct our own personal credo, as if faith were not a gift from God. This is fostered by humanistic concepts, by the naive presumption that religion, like government, can be regulated by man, and by a misinterpretation of the democratic principle of freedom of religion. It is especially appealing to young people who pride themselves on intellectual talents, for it stamps them in their own eyes as independent thinkers.

Another snare is the deification of the word "faith," its use as a wonder-working invocation, completely independent of its Object. It is responsible for a blind optimism and also for such vapid monstrosities as the current popular song *I Believe*, which brings faith down to the level of a mawkish mood. Romantic youngsters are likely to be carried away by such sentimental delusion.

Parents are not immune to the various toxins that permeate our atmosphere. With them, the infection is likely to have become chronic, part and parcel of the way of life they transmit to their children.

One particularly American error is the heresy of hyperactivity. In teaching their children the value of work, of making profitable use of their time and energies, they exaggerate the importance of purposeful activity, and measure the importance of a person by what he can do. They rank achievement, *doing*, above virtue, *being*. While man must work to live, he was not made for work, nor for the impersonal goods that result from work. If youngsters are subjected to this false attitude to the point where it prevents their fulfilling their true vocation—the adoration of God and the love of those about them—their faith will shrivel, for the god of things requires no faith—only slavery. If, on the other hand, they rebel against this bondage, they may also rebel against the religion professed by those who preach it as if it were Catholic doctrine.

Overindulgence

To go to the opposite extreme, solicitude for their childrens' happiness makes some parents overindulgent, eager to gratify, not only afraid to punish them, but fearful of letting them spend themselves in anything that requires abnegation. This is perhaps the most common fault, and it ranges from apologetic deference to the modern preoccupation with pleasure and comfort, to a tigerish determination to stand between their children and any menacing trouble. Because they are "sacrificing" themselves for their children, they delude themselves into thinking they are being good parents. In reality they are creating quicksands of selfishness and greed, cultivating an all-consuming soil in which no faith can grow. But it sometimes happens that their children feel, with Claudel, that youth "is not meant for pleasure but for heroism," and, finding no outlet for self-abnegation in the religion their parents avow, they turn to one that makes demands of them. They are ripe for communism or any other ism that will accept a measure of self-surrender from them.

Responsibility of Teachers

Sometimes it is not parents, but teachers, who infect children with doubt. At no age do children need a teacher more that during adolescence, for at this time they are turning from their familiar world to explore a world unknown, and they need a guide, a competent authority on the tremendous questions that are teeming within them. The right teacher at this time can point out stimulating heights to be scaled and inspire them with the confidence they need to reach these heights.

No one disputes that nuns or brothers who teach in high schools must meet exacting standards, first because much is expected of one who has dedicated his life to God, and secondly because they have to deal not with the easy, all-accepting trustfulness of little children, but with the critical appraisal of adolescents, who, while looking for perfection, are eager to pounce on every fault. And yet I am confident that many of the complaints made by fallen-away Catholics attributing their apostasy to class-room injustices are post-mortem rationalizations. Most children, especially those from large families, are too familiar with outbursts of human frailty even in homes where perfection is genuinely pursued to be deeply scandalized by its presence in the classroom.

What really causes damage is a tendency to stress non-essentials at the expense of the essential purpose of Catholic education: the formation of enlightened, apostolic Christians. Part of this is due to the necessity of keeping up with the requirements of state regents, and meeting the scholastic standards of secular schools. Part of it is due to the need to gratify the ambition of parents who look upon education as a means of rising in the world. Some of it is due to a provincialism which identifies Christianity with Americanism, and attempts to vindicate it by its material achievements.

The dreary list of tacit fallacies and quasi-heretical practices can go on indefinitely: the use of religion as a means to a finite end; the confusion between patriotism, which is Christian charity put to civic practice, and nationalism, which is worship of state; superstitions under many guises; snobbery in any form; etc., etc. The point is that adolescence is the age at which children are capable of piercing through sham and hypocrisy. It is very possible that in spite of the errors of their parents and teachers they will see enough of the glory of Christianity to want to embrace it in all its purity. On the other hand, there is the danger that they will not only reject their parents' error, but with it the entire content of their Christian heritage. Or there is the alternative that they will accept the defective religion they're given because life is easier that way, and so continue the process of the corruption of Christianity.

Theology for Parents

Parents dare not offer their children anything less than the truth. This does not mean that they have to be theologians. But their knowledge of their faith should at least be commensurate with the general level of their scholastic attainments. If it is not, they should be sufficiently interested and humble to be willing to repair the omission even now. So that they can help their children cope with doubt and confusion and misinformation. The worst thing they can do is try to justify their ignorance and even to make a virtue of it. "I trust the Church enough to believe whatever she teaches without having to have it proved," is a laudable attitude when there is no access to learning. In these days of universal literacy, and when the Church is being attacked from so many different positions, such an attitude smacks of intellectual and spiritual sloth. It may even give scandal to a youngster whose inner powers are just awakening to the lie of the intellect.

Long before modern psychology dissected and analyzed the adolescent mind, the Bishops of the Church in many countries designated the onset of adolescence as an appropriate time for the rebirth of the spirit marked by the sacrament of Confirmation. What happens to a child's faith between the ages of twelve and eighteen will be difficult to eradicate, for it is at this time that it sinks deep roots into the wellsprings of personality. In chosen souls it has born ripe fruit at this age. Catholic hagiology is full of teen-age saints and martyrs. According to tradition, Our Lady herself became God's mother at sixteen, and Christ made formal profession of His dedication to His Father's business at twelve. Certainly these are indications of how precious these years are to God.

It is important, during this period, to safeguard the faith from every danger. But this negative precaution is not sufficient. The faith must also be nourished. Not all the lost faith of our youth can be laid to corruption and violence. Much of it is choked by inertia.

Need for Action

Faith is made strong by the active exercise of virtue. St. James says of Abraham that "faith did co-operate with his works and by works faith was made perfect."

Adolescence flowers with its own special virtues: generosity of soul, a capacity for spontaneous response to beauty in nature and in art, the spirit of adventure, and a soaring, yearning reaching out for the things of God. St. Augustine, recalling his own youth, writes: "O Truth, Truth, how inwardly did the very marrow of my soul pant for You."

These special virtues need to be kept in practice. The active virtues, generosity of soul and the spirit of adventure, are exercised by the corporal works of mercy, by service and self-denial, by discipline and sacrifice. Adolescents are tireless advocates of great causes, and nothing thrills them more than the challenge of difficult projects. Fortunate is the youth whose parents ask great things of him, and while commending the progress he is making, point to still higher objectives. It is often the lack of any sort of direction, the frustration of the spirit of adventure that leads the young to turn to delinquency, to perpetuate a sort of wry justice and force the attention of a preoccupied and indifferent world. Many communities are beginning to provide intelligent outlets for this passion for enterprise through Catholic Action. In one community they are giving the time to cleaning, repairing and painting the run-down homes in the neighborhood, as an organized service. There is a great need for young high school girls to give voluntary help in homes where there are many children and no money to pay a baby sitter. Some of the parish sodalities could make this one of their social activities.

Reverence for Beauty

The ability to respond to the beauty of goods endowed with values which communicate deep and eternal truths is one of man's highest endowments. It sees beauty not as a superfluous decoration for matter, but as an integral value in a created thing which evokes the image of its Creator, and whose message is *Sursum Corda*. It is essential that parents try to cultivate this quality in their children and keep it from being blunted by the violent assaults that movies and TV make on the imagination, and by the wear and tear of the exterior traffic of the senses. How can their children be expected to aspire to Unknown Beauty if they are unable to appreciate Its reflection which is accessible to them in nature, music, poetry, and great art?

Prayer

Finally we come to that which comes first of all—the life of prayer. Many parents who think they have started out auspiciously, with little tots kneeling at mother's knee and lisping their bedtime prayers, wonder why their teen-aged children break away from this practice. Of course, it is the whole infantile atmosphere of this kind of prayer that revolts the adolescent, plus the connotation that adults do not have to pray, but just sit and listen.

Family prayer should be something that is a privilege to participate in, and also something to grow up to. Let father and mother take the leading part. Let the children's share be small when they are little—an Our Father, a Hail Mary, whatever they can manage. But let them see and feel that this is a time of great dignity and seriousness. *It is more important for the parents to pray themselves than to police the children during prayer time.*

Families have a rich storehouse of prayer in the Church to select from and *adapt to their own needs.* They might recite the Rosary together, or part of the Divine Office, such as Compline, in the evening.

The important thing, of course, is not so much the time spent on prayer, as the atmosphere of prayer in the home. And this atmosphere cannot be created by merely filling the home with the physical appurtenances of religion. As the Mystical Body in miniature, the Christian home is permeated with the breath of the living Christ. Parents can impose the externals of their faith only as long as their authority is accepted. Their enduring testament is the inner spark of faith which they ignite in their children, and this must be struck from the flame of their own unshakable convictions which, of necessity, illuminates everything they do.

THE DATING SYSTEM

DOROTHY X. DIX

It is only at rare and awful moments in history that God is excluded from human society. When that happens, as it has happened in our day, one can expect to find the very roots of the social order disjointed and perverted. That is why contemporary Christians have to be radicals. It may be unpleasant to learn that you have built your economic or social or political life on sand, but it is better to learn it sooner than later, if it is true. It should be a consolation anyhow to discover how badly the world fares without God. In this article we are going to consider one of the favorite pillars of secular social life: the dating system.

It Is Based on a False Principle

As competition is to the economic system (that is, the false principle upon which it rests), so is the dating system to the social life of our youth. Let us first get straight what dating is. Dating is the prevailing system in America for meeting and mating, that is, for the social life of unmarried but marriageable people. Its essence is the pairing off of couples for unchaperoned activity of whatever sort. It stands in opposition to a variety of other systems formerly or currently in effect here and elsewhere. It is useful to mention some of these other systems by way of contrast. In some pagan countries it is the custom for unmarried girls to be completely isolated from young men until the day (at an early age) when they are married to husbands of their parents' choice. In Latin-American countries a system of chaperonage prevails, young girls being allowed to attend some social functions with eligible and carefully selected young men, but always accompanied by an adult, although some privacy is allowed to engaged couples. Our tradition (antedating) has been largely that of the family and church gatherings where young people met and mixed informally in groups, usually while participating in some vigorous activity like folk dancing. The dating system is different essentially from all of these. It means a pairing off of one girl with one boy when both are of marriageable age, physically anyhow. If there happen to be parents around, or if it is a double or a triple date, or if adolescents sometimes gather in large groups, these are accidental variations on the system and do not change its essence, although they may modify its effects.

Any system of mixed social life for unmarried young men and women must be judged by whether or not it conduces to good marriages, and it is on this basis that dating must be regarded as an unfortunate system. It is important to see that dating must be judged in the light of future marriage. It cannot be considered the same as the casual recreation of boys and girls who have not yet reached adolescence, simply because adolescence changes radically the physical and psychological relationship between the sexes. Nor can dating be considered as leading nowhere in particular. Marriage is the adult and stable state to which all post-adolescent relations between the sexes normally tend. Whether or not those dating consider their actions in the light of matrimony is beside the point; the system remains auxiliary to matrimony as its natural end.

Dating Is Not a Good Way to Choose a Mate

The goal in finding a husband or wife is to come out with the *one* person best suited to oneself. Normally there should be a process of selection based on common and casual activity with a likely group (of similar age, background, religion and education). One's interest normally will narrow to a few and finally to *one* as a suitable time for marriage approaches. The intimacy and isolation of dates is not necessary until the engagement period. Dating works backwards. It offers *one* to begin with, who need not necessarily be suitable in any way. (We are thinking particularly of girls here. Their parents don't choose their dates for them and when they are off at school or college or work, they meet someone through a blind date or because he's sitting at the next desk and it's only by chance that he would have a similar background or tastes.) As far as the dating system is concerned one might be going around with that one the rest of one's life. There is nothing in the system itself which allows for meeting other eligible young men or women. Accidentally, however, one might meet someone else's date and take up with him or her, or one might start the whole process over again with whoever is sitting at the desk on the other side or with another blind date. Most young people acquire some assortment of occasional dates before long but that does not mean necessarily that they have on hand a string of potential husbands or wives; more often it is a case of acquiring a series of acquaintances of the opposite sex, no one of whom, for this reason or that, is a serious matrimonial prospect.

Besides narrowing down from the beginning something which should be selective, dating is further exclusive in that it is a competitive affair. Some girls (and boys) have all the dates, while others who look less like Lana Turner or who haven't got what it takes to shine in an atmosphere of juke boxes and drug store cokes are cruelly neglected. If the qualities which would make a girl a popular date were the same qualities which make her a good wife and mother, or if male popularity were a reflection of Christian manliness and presaged future good "husbandry," then there would be some excuse for the poignant suffering inflicted on those who, at a sensitive age, do not make the grade of popular appeal. As things stand, however, it is hard to see how Christian youth can justify excluding so many as it does from what should be their normal fun.

The Dating System Is an Occasion of Sin

Despite its Kinsey Reports, contemporary America may go down in history as our most naive period, that is, naive about the very things in which its citizens profess to be knowing and sophisticated—chiefly sex. Someone must know what it's all about but the ordinary citizen doesn't see the connection between advertising art and adultery, the dichotomy between *Life* magazine's photography and its earnest editorials, the ratio between immodest dress and fornication, or the cause and effect relationship between the dating system and sins of impurity.

Physical attraction between a young man and a young woman is a mere matter of chemistry, and the compound can be formed of almost any chance elements. Knowing this, other generations have conspired to keep young people at a fairly considerable distance from each other until a harmony was attained between them on the spiritual, intellectual and practical basis. They knew that physical harmony would follow quickly and easily, and favored early marriages with fairly short engagements. Nowadays parents allow their thirteen-year old daughters to go "steady" and carefully leave home when the young folks are throwing a party there. They have no real right to be astonished at any of the consequences which result.

It is possible to go on dates without committing sins of impurity but there is no evidence whatever that this is the usual case. The circumstances of dating invite impurity; both in the essential circumstance which is the pairing off (it makes little difference here whether it is a single or a double date, for there is a code of dating ethics which demands scrupulous disregard by the couples of each other), and in the accidental circumstances of automobiles, suggestive movies and drinking.

One of the most tragic situations today is that of young married couples who already hate each other and are ready for divorce at twenty-one. They are the victims of "chemical explosions," often date-induced. They "fell for each other" physically (it is so easy) before they had an opportunity to explore each other's minds or characters, much less the depths of each other's souls, and after the chemical action set in, it was too late to learn anything else. Love of that sort distorts all judgments. Unfortunately, chemistry doesn't stand up long under the realities of married life. One day its charm is suddenly gone, and the bride and groom face a life which will be a real martyrdom if they are to save their souls.

Other Unlovely Effects of the Dating System

The dating system is not only unsuited to marriage as an end, but it doesn't even profess to be directed toward marriage. Few boys want to take a girl out if she is looking for a husband, and yet she should be looking for a husband, and he for a wife. One still finds the tradition among some of the Irish of not going out (more than once or twice anyhow) with someone whom one doesn't intend to marry. There is much to be said for this stand, which regards matrimony very seriously.

The dating system probably has a worse effect on girls than it does on boys. It is no disgrace for a man if he doesn't date, and so the more serious ones just don't. Either they find a girl in the course of their work or study whom they wish to marry, and quietly go out with her until such time as they can marry or they abstain entirely from dating while young. It would be interesting to see how many of today's prominent men were prominent dates in college or high school. Probably their prominence reflects time well and seriously spent in their formative years. It would be useful also to interview the wives of men who dated much in their youth (Has your husband learned to fix furnaces yet? Is he making full use of the talents God gave him? Is it any fun to live with a "life of the party"? Does he have difficulty with fidelity?) It has always been evident to everyone except those who most need to know that the smoothest dates usually make the worst mates.

But the effect of the dating system on girls is worse than it is on boys; the more popular the girl, the worse the effect. If Susie starts dating at thirteen or fifteen or whenever they start now, is very popular and doesn't get married until she is twenty-two, she will have had the opportunity to have gone through the preliminaries of the preliminaries of marriage with several hundred boys and men in that time. Let us suppose that Susie is a determinedly virtuous girl, which is quite a gratuitous assumption these days. Even so, she will have become skilled at the art of superficially attracting men, at making largely nonsensical conversation, at entertaining an assortment of vacant-headed young men, and at warding off innumerable threats to her purity. Her vanity will have been given every opportunity to turn her whole nature toward a self-love which is the worst possible basis of marriage.

Some of these ill-effects are generally recognized. There is another which escapes almost everyone's attention: the supreme waste of time which dating involves—whether in dating itself or in preparing for dates or scheming to date or discussing dates. A person's whole youth passes in this curiously inept process of *choosing* a mate. Where is any consideration given at all to *preparing* to make a good husband or wife?

Getting Rid of the Dating System

Dating as a system has obscure origins. The laxity of parents, big-city life, modern dancing and music, small apartments, and the commercialization of recreation are doubtless all contributory factors. But the remote genesis must have been spiritual, involving a moral and intellectual decline, a perversion of religion and then a revulsion from it. Certain it is in any case that only a spiritual reconstruction can change it now.

The new Christian families which are being formed may never come to blows with the dating system. Their homes will respond to the rhythm of the liturgical year, their children will be formed apostolically from early childhood, and probably grow up to marry other first fruits of the lay apostolate.

• The problem, then, does not center around the next generation but around this generation. It focuses on the teenagers and bobby soxers who have been nurtured on cokes and comics, movies and name bands; who have been led by

Hollywood and mass circulation magazines to believe themselves the final flowering of emancipation, the lovely end product of progress. It is for their sakes that the dating system should be changed but it is also by *them* that it must be changed, for their parents lack the authority, the desire and the basis for corporate action.

It will not be hard to change the dating system if young people want it changed, but they have fallen into the habit of thinking they are *privileged* to go on dates, instead of realizing how they are betrayed by the system. Any serious move by a group of adolescent leaders (say a Catholic Action ferment) will work for the demolition of the system. Suppose such a group were to consider seriously the goal of marriage. Any study on the subject (say of the Church's teaching, or a poll of young married people in their neighborhood to see if they were happy and, if not, why not) would serve to bring dating into perspective. They would soon see that marriage is not "one long date" as the advertisers more or less suggest, but that it is a serious and marvelous adventure to which dating is a poor prelude.

Let's suppose that our hypothetical teen-agers were to make a serious study of "unselfishness" in school. Surely they would discover that dating conduces to the happiness of the very few. If, then, they were to set about, as a project, to try to make *all* their classmates happy and have common fun, they would find themselves doing away with the dating system.

A similar effect would follow any honest inquiry into adolescent morality. It would be discovered that youthful casuistry (which knows the hairline beyond which venial sin begins, and can stipulate exactly the border between venial and mortal sin) is not the highway to purity. They would discover how useful it is to divert youthful attention to matters apostolic and wholesome.

Once there is Christian conviction in the matter it will be easy to change the pillars of social life. Then the parochial parties sponsored by the churches will take on a Christian orientation (and not seem, as they often do, an ecclesiastical sponsorship of secular and pagan festivities). Then family and house parties will be stimulated again. Then folk dancing will be seen for the wholesome fun that it is (and the more Christian and graceful dances will be learned). We may even hope that the blatant and hideous noises which emerge from juke boxes will begin to offend youthful ears. (One of the interesting minor phenomena of our time is the transformation of the appearance of juke boxes to conform more and more to the way they sound—sort of hellish).

A Final Word

It does not follow from the fact that the dating system is essentially inept, and an occasion of sin, that everyone has to stop dating forthwith. Boy must still meet girl, and the way to reform social life is not to drop out of it altogether. But let those who date realize what they are about and work toward structural reforms in the social system.